REFORMATION

NOT

REVOLUTION

We unquestionably live in an age of revolution; of revolt against God, His Word, and His created order. The voice of progressivism tells us that the forces of liberalism, secularism, and further revolution are not only inevitable, but good. Many Christians live under the imposing shadow of these forces, instinctively aware that they are opposed to Christ, yet unsure of how to chart a more faithful path forward. In this book, Dave Forsythe introduces the lay churchman to classical Christian thinking. While clearly giving ultimate authority to God's inerrant word, and its expression in the form of confessional Protestant theology, Forsythe also weaves in historical developments. While it may be easy for Christians to despair, and to believe the progressive assumption that their vision of history is inevitable, the reader should be challenged to think of how the Christian order, now under attack, even came to be in the first place? Did the classical world, along with its law tradition and cultures, develop in a vacuum? Or are these enduring evidences of what can be built when Christians faithfully apply God's law-word to the real world around them? By what standard are we to evaluate moral, spiritual, and legal claims? As a fellow classical, confessional, and Reformed Christian, I am pleased to share the author's answer – by the standard of God's Holy Scriptures.

Matthew F. Plett (MATS – Whitefield Theological Seminary)
PASTOR, TRINITY FELLOWSHIP, NIVERVILLE, MB

This work offers a profound and timely critique of the cultural upheavals shaping our world, grounded firmly in a historic, robust biblical worldview. It's a compelling call to reclaim God's law as the very essence of divine authority, challenging believers to re-engage the public square with clarity and courage.

Rev. Dr. Uri Brito
SENIOR PASTOR, PROVIDENCE CHURCH, PENSACOLA, FL
PRESIDING MINISTER, COMMUNION OF REFORMED EVANGELICAL CHURCHES

David Forsythe has offered an excellent summary and defense of the theonomic interpretation of God's law for today's Christians. He takes God's law with utmost seriousness as, indeed, every saint in the biblical canon and the vast majority until well into the 19th century did. Since then, pietism and dispensationalism have tended to erode this pervasive confidence in the abiding authority of God's law, and kudos to David for his skillful attempt to revive it. While God's law-abiding Christians might not agree with every detail of his application, the case he lays out for the continuing authority of God's law is superb and worth every Christian's consideration.

P. Andrew Sandlin
FOUNDER & PRESIDENT AT THE CENTER FOR CULTURAL LEADERSHIP

I wholeheartedly endorse this bold and principled contribution to the conversation on authority and ethics in the civil sphere. Rooted in years of missionary experience, sharpened by deep worldview formation, and tested in the public arena of political candidacy, Dave Forsythe brings a rare combination of conviction, courage, and clarity. His unwavering commitment to the Lordship of Christ over all of life—especially in the realm of politics—is both refreshing and necessary in our time. This work stands as a compelling call for Christians to think biblically about the state, and to recover a vision of civil government under the crown rights of King Jesus.

Steven R. Martins
DIRECTOR OF THE CÁNTARO INSTITUTE
FOUNDING PASTOR OF SEVILLA CHAPEL, ST. CATHARINES, ONTARIO, CANADA

REFORMATION *NOT* REVOLUTION

WHY GOD'S LAW MATTERS FOR SOCIETY

DAVID A. FORSYTHE

DEDICATION

To Andrew DeBartolo and Matthew Hallick.
May the Canadian church rise up to be half as brave as you've been
in the public square for Christ.

TABLE OF CONTENTS

FOREWORD

It is a happy providence when a fresh voice enters the public square with the courage to speak plainly, faithfully and unapologetically where polite evasions now reign. In my recent book, *Ruler of Kings*, I argued that Christ's mediatorial authority extends, unequivocally, to every sphere of human life and that the civil order is no exception. David Forsythe has taken up that vital theme and carried it further, offering in these pages a bracing—yet pastoral—call to reformation, not revolution. His central thesis is as old as the Scriptures and yet as contemporary as tomorrow morning's headlines: the law-Word of God is not a museum piece for the painstaking scrutiny of antiquarians, but the charter of human flourishing. Where it is kept, liberty and justice grow; where it is despised, bondage follows.

David is no armchair theologian, but writes as a man who has tasted both the promises and the perils of public office. He has stood on the hustings, knocked on doors, and felt the icy stare of secular orthodoxy. Out of that furnace of testing he brings not the cynicism of the defeated but the steel of the convicted and persuaded. His analysis is richly biblical, historically informed, and unapologetically Kuyperian in its insistence that every square inch already belongs to Christ the King. Yet he avoids the sterile and non-committal abstractions of ivory-tower scholarship. Here are concrete questions—about law, family, church, and state—met with equally concrete answers rooted in the whole counsel of God.

Some will find his proposals unfashionable; but all who truly love the Lord will find them unflinchingly faithful. David reminds us that the alternative to God's righteous precepts is never a neutral space but another law, another sovereignty, another god. The very choice before Elijah's Israel—If Yahweh is God, follow Him—stands before our own civilization with renewed urgency. In setting forth the abiding validity and social necessity of God's law, the author joins a noble company: Knox and Rutherford, Kuyper and Bavinck, Van Til and Rushdoony. He does so, however, in a register uniquely suited to our Canadian moment—a moment when the West is fast discovering that a people cannot sow cultural apostasy and reap civil peace and liberty.

Read this book, then, with an open Bible and an open mind. Agree or disagree with David's every conclusion, you will be compelled to think—seriously—about the only kind of renewal that can withstand the gathering storm: reformation according to the Word of God. May the church heed the call, and may Christ be pleased to crown such obedience with revival.

Solus Christus,

Rev. Dr. Joseph Boot

President and Founder, Ezra Institute

ACKNOWLEDGMENTS

It is with tremendous gratitude that I now honor those who contributed to the writing of this work. First of all, many thanks to my sweet wife, Alyssa, who painstakingly proofread my manuscript for any and all spelling and grammatical errors. Secondly, I wish to extend my sincere appreciation to my good friend Philippe Loyer for his insights into making my line of argumentation consistent and coherent. Furthermore, I'd like to offer my heartfelt thanks to my editor, Rebekah Tysoe, for all her meticulous work in this project. Finally, I would like to express my deep gratitude to Dr. Rev. Michael Thiessen for his encouragement in this work.

PREFACE

Most Canadians can say they have had the opportunity to vote in either a federal, provincial, or municipal election, but few can say they have had the opportunity to run in one. In the Lord's kind providence, I had the privilege of serving my community in a way I never thought I would—I ran for the office of Member of Provincial Parliament (MPP) in the June 2022 Ontario provincial election.

It all began in a Tim Hortons while having coffee with a dear friend. I had recently lost my job, I had a shoulder injury, and I was in the process of charting the way forward to provide for my young family of six. Suddenly, my friend suggested that I investigate the possibility of running with the Ontario Party, a fairly new socially conservative provincial party. Initially, I thought he was joking…but he wasn't.

You see, my family and I had served for three years as missionaries in Central Africa, working together with a local denomination in evangelism and discipleship, and we had come to realize the importance of thinking at a foundational worldview level. As we sought to minister to our Central African friends, we were forced to push our understanding of authority and ethics into the corners, realizing that we needed a full-orbed, consistent biblical world-and-life-view in order to communicate the truths of God's Word effectively. Likewise, we needed to grasp their traditional African worldview in order to understand how what we were saying was being interpreted—all while attempting to comprehend their culture—so we could address the idols of their culture with the law and the gospel. What this fundamental reorientation in our thinking accomplished was creating a mindset of "All of Christ for all of life for all the world!" This led me to become increasingly interested in the civil sphere, and law and politics. Culture is the manifestation of the worship of the masses in the public square, and politics is the process of legislating morality on particular cultural issues. In other words, "Culture shapes politics, and religion is at the root of culture," as Richard Neuhaus once aptly put it.[1] This has become a real passion in my life—that Jesus really is Lord over all and His gospel really does have the power to take back everything the enemy stole, and not just a few souls here and there. My

---

[1] R.R. Reno, *Religion, Culture, and Public Life,* https://www.firstthings.com/article/2009/04/021-religion-culture-and-public-life.

greatest longing is to see all of life, indeed all the nations, progressively come under the rule of King Jesus as He transforms the hearts and lives of the multitudes, by His Spirit and as the preaching of His law and gospel go forth.

Having been a faithful friend for many years, and so knowing these things, my brother in the Lord encouraged me to apply to the Ontario Party in order to begin dialoguing with their staff. Upon discerning that this would be a good fit, and having been officially offered candidacy within the party, my wife and I discussed, prayed, and decided to step out in faith on the basis of Matthew 6:33 which says, "But seek first the kingdom of God and His righteousness [justice], and all these things will be added to you." And this is exactly what we did.

Throughout my entire campaign leading up to and including the election in June, I openly ran as a Christian, putting into practice all that I had learned about the importance of worldview. I intentionally approached every issue and every conversation, whether at a rally or at the door, from the standpoint of Proverbs 26:4-5, "Answer not a fool according to his folly, lest you be like him yourself. Answer a fool according to his folly, lest he be wise in his own eyes." In other words, "Don't give up the Word of God as your grounds of authority, or else you'll become a fool too. But, for the sake of showing the fool his folly, step into his worldview for a moment to provide the internal critique." Thus, for every position I took on policy—whether it be in protecting all human life (from conception to natural death) or in opposing the digital ID and currency program—I made sure I had thought through the relevant biblical passages ahead of time so as to consistently argue from the standpoint of Holy Scripture and not mere political preference. Though I certainly didn't do this perfectly at every point throughout my campaign, I can honestly say that with the help of the Holy Spirit, I stood firm for Christ in the public square, bearing witness to the goodness of His righteous and just standards and the glory of His name. I can also say that I've learned much about living as a consistent Christian in the civil sphere in contrast to sheer defeatism on the one hand, and deceitful self-advancement on the other. May the Lord be praised for His work in my life, as well as the lives of many others, through this effort.

In light of these things, I'm now writing to contribute to the conversation on authority and ethics, particularly as it impacts the civil sphere. This is in no way to minimize the importance of other Christ-delegated institutions of limited authority, such as the family and the local congregation. Rather, I wish to focus our attention upon a particular sphere of society, which receives very little exegetically-based thought and attention among modern evangelicals—that sphere being the state. I believe the recent years of 2020-2022 have served the church well to remind her of the absolute necessity of having a thorough grasp on the doctrine which Abraham Kuyper called *sphere sovereignty*. This work is meant to complement Dr. Joseph Boot's work, *Ruler of Kings*,[2] in the effort to recover a biblically driven vision for law and politics under

---

[2] Joseph Boot, *Ruler of Kings: Toward a Christian Vision of Government*, London: Wilberforce Publications, 2022.

the kingdom rule of Christ. May the Lord be honored and His people benefited through this work.

David A. Forsythe

Selkirk, Manitoba, Canada

CHAPTER 1

A LAW WORTH KEEPING

Here in the West, we're living in the midst of a highly fluctuating context with moment-to-moment changes in direct orders coming from the top. The goal of this radical cultural revolution in which we find ourselves is to transform society based on principles radically different from those previously known. This is evident in the UN Women's visualization of their utopian community, *Equiterra*,[1] which envisions a totally egalitarian society, whether it be on the economic, ethnic, gender, religious, or physical ability front. Likewise, we saw this cultural Marxist

---

[1] UN Women Australia, *Welcome to Equiterra, Where Gender Equality Is Real*, 18 March 2020, <https://unwomen.org.au/welcome-to-equiterra-where-gender-equality-is-real>.

vision in the Canadian logo stating, "Hate Has No Home Here,"[2] which began appearing in front yards in the place of Canadian flags in the days surrounding Canada Day, July 1, 2021. Since that time, the same logo has become a kind of advertisement for the Left on the rear bumpers of supporters' cars, along with other such revolutionary logos. For many followers of Christ these fundamental societal shifts have been extremely disorienting and overwhelming. Why? Just as Christians over the course of the past 120 years have progressively abandoned the public square, we've also abandoned thinking through everyday issues in light of a robust, thoroughgoing biblical worldview. This can be seen especially in the shift away from the systematic preaching of God's law in the modern pulpit, resulting in an antinomian-minded generation of believers who are highly susceptible to being carried along by the collective reasoning of a society filled with self-actualizing individuals. The reality that ungodly image bearers don't stop finding ways to turn creation into culture that rebels against God is as plain as the nose on one's face. Just because conservative Christians have come to believe that engaging in the culture is somehow "liberal" in and of itself and that a privatized, ecclesiasticized form of religion is the way to go does not make it so. As Greg Bahnsen once said, "There is no neutrality."[3] I would therefore like to suggest that the only way to make sense of the revolution in which we

---

[2] Barrie Today, Shawn Gibson, *Barrie Families Unite Launches Anti-Hate Sign Campaign*, 24 June 2021, <https://www.barrietoday.com/local-news/barrie-families-unite-launches-anti-hate-sign-campaign-3904175>.

[3] David Bahnsen, in quoting his father, Greg. Greg L. Bahnsen, *By This Standard: The Authority of God's Law Today*, Nacogdoches, TX: Covenant Media Press, 2008, Kindle Location 39.

find ourselves is to provide a consistent apologetic to the false ideas being promoted as the "right thing" for the "common good." Additionally, we must begin re-engaging as the cultural leaders in the public square as we've been created to be, returning to a full-orbed understanding of God's law and how it applies to us today.

A HISTORIC APPROACH

The seventeenth-century English Puritans were the direct spiritual descendants of the Protestant Reformation in mainland Europe, particularly as it manifested itself in Geneva under the study, instruction, and leadership of John Calvin. Among those trained under his tutelage was John Knox, a sixteenth-century Scotsman, who eventually took the Reformation back to Scotland. Over time, this led to the formation of the Covenanters and the beginning of the Church of Scotland. Simultaneously, as the Reformation moved south in the British Isles, many within the Church of England were persuaded by Scripture, and thus moved away from an Anglo-Catholic viewpoint. Indeed, the Thirty-Nine Articles of the Church of England (1571) can be counted as a historic Reformed confession. Upon the passing of the Act of Uniformity (1558), brought about by Elizabeth I, thousands of clergy and laity were forced out of the state church over biblically held convictions. These original Nonconformists began calling themselves Presbyterians in keeping with Knox's elder-rule view of church government, one involving church councils. Some well-known seventeenth-century Presbyterian preachers would be Samuel Rutherford, Matthew Henry, and John

Flavel. As Presbyterian scholars continued to study Scripture, some began arguing instead for an elder-led model contained within the individual congregation. Church leaders and congregations following this distinction became known as Congregationalists. Some significant leaders in this stream of Puritanism were John Owen, Oliver Cromwell, and Thomas Goodwin. The final group came as the result of certain Congregational men re-examining church polity and practice within the context of their understanding of the covenant of grace. This version of Congregationalists called themselves Baptists, since they had come to the conclusion that only those with a credible profession of faith in Christ ought to be baptized and so enter into the membership of the local covenant community. Some noteworthy seventeenth-century Particular Baptists were John Spilsbury, John Bunyan, and Nehemiah Coxe.[4]

In terms of Reformed ethics, what comes to mind for those most familiar with them is a hermeneutic that says, "Unless explicitly altered in some way in the Newer Testament by Christ or His apostles, laws given in the Older Testament continue to apply to us today." This principle of interpretation was universally held amongst the Covenanters and Puritans in their confessions, whether they be Presbyterian, Congregationalist, or Baptist. Chapter Nineteen of the Westminster Confession of Faith (1647) (WCF) applies this principle in its explanation that it is the moral law, along with the general equity (fundamental principles) of

---

[4] See Pascal Denault, *The Distinctiveness of Baptist Covenant Theology: A Comparison Between Seventeenth-Century Particular Baptist and Paedobaptist Federalism,* Birmingham, AL: Solid Ground Christian Books, 2013.

its civil applications, which is perpetually binding and incumbent on all men everywhere.

In this way, this historic Puritan hermeneutic helps to safeguard biblical ethics from straying off in the Anabaptist direction, which cuts off the entire Older Testament (OT) on the ethical front and makes Newer Testament ethics exclusive to believers, and only in a privatized, ecclesiasticized sense at that. In other words, a consistent application of the Reformed hermeneutic of *analogia fide (analogy of faith)*—which teaches that later revelation is given to interpret, explain, and apply former revelation to biblical ethics—safeguards against various and sundry types of antinomianism.

GOD HIMSELF IS THE LAW

As with all doctrines, the Puritans began with the nature of God. Near the beginning of the WCF, Chapter Two opens with these words, "There is but one only living and true God, who is infinite in being and perfection, a most pure spirit, invisible, without body, parts, or passions...." Indeed, God is not the end result of a giant God-making project. We cannot think of each of Yahweh's attributes as individual components that were assembled together by someone else the way engineers and mechanics might assemble together millions of well-made parts in order to construct a jumbo jet or a container ship. Nor can we think of Yahweh as lacking anything so that He might reach into some giant cosmic bag to pull out the appropriate attributes He needs. Nor can we think of Him as one Spirit among many, even the most powerful, within the broader category of "divine." No! God Himself is the definition of pure divinity. There is no difference between His existence as a most pure Being and His essence as a most pure Being—with Him, they are one and the same. Likewise, God Himself is the definition of pure love, pure holiness, pure sovereignty, and pure wisdom. Truly, there is no difference between His attributes and His essence—with Him, the two are one and the same. Nevertheless, His attributes are somehow mysteriously distinguishable from one another, just as the Scriptures treat them. Furthermore, Yahweh is entirely self-sufficient in and of Himself, lacking nothing, and eternally existing as such. Indeed, this is what He meant when He revealed His covenant name *Yahweh*—"I AM WHO I AM" —to Moses in the wilderness (cf. Exodus 3:13ff).

What this means is that God's law is not something distinct from Himself, which He arbitrarily developed for His creatures to obey. This would put Yahweh in the same category as the god of Islam. Because Yahweh is One (cf. Deuteronomy 6:4), just as in and of Himself He *is* love, He Himself likewise *is* the moral standard. Each and every imperative He gives to man is a direct extension and expression of Himself. Each and every moral requirement, whether naturally placed in man or codified in His Word, is an expression of God Himself. Therefore to rebel against the law is to rebel against the Law-Giver directly. Likewise, to obey His law is to obey Him directly. Why? God did not imagine and then proffer His own law—He Himself is the law!

CREATED AFTER GOD'S LIKENESS

Building on this, WCF, Chapter Four Paragraph Two explains:

> …endued with knowledge, righteousness, and true holiness, after his own image, having the law of God written in their hearts, and power to fulfil it; and yet under a possibility of transgressing it, being left to the liberty of their own will, which was subject unto change.

In typical Puritan fashion, the framers of the Confession strove to understand earlier texts—in this case, Genesis 1:27—in the light that later texts shed on them. For example, in Romans Chapter Two, St. Paul insists that, while Jews are condemned by the law they received through Moses, Gentiles are also condemned, since "they show that the work of the law is written on their hearts, while their conscience also bears witness" (vs. 14-15). His point is twofold. First, he wants his readers to understand that the content of the law for both Jews and non-Jews is the same. At this juncture the point is implied, yet a few verses later what was implicit becomes explicit as the apostle refers back to the Ten Commandments (cf. vs. 21-24). Second, he explains that the law written on the heart came first and is natural, since it even holds Gentiles to account before God by impressing itself on their consciences, though they never received the codified version of it as did the Jews.

What this means is that prior to the fall, Adam and Eve knew God's law intuitively since it was written in their hearts. They were image bearers in God's good world. Mankind could not escape living in His presence, walking with Him in intimate fellowship day by day. They could therefore not possibly escape thinking in terms of God's law as they sought to fulfill the dominion mandate. Everything from how to treat each other in marital covenant, to creating cultural artifacts and practices—like food, tools, and music—to bearing children and training them to do the same, was governed, ordered, and motivated by His good statutes. Our first parents knew very well that obedience to their Creator's ordinances was not merely a matter of personal piety. It was also a matter of cultural piety, as they were meant to gradually transform creation into godly culture, reflecting back to Yahweh—His holiness, beauty, and sovereignty. Thus, love for God and love for neighbor had value and was meant to make its way into the nooks and crannies of everyday life in very practical ways. Indeed, this image-of-God-infused mandate did not fundamentally change with the fall. It was rather added and reaffirmed, in order to include the need for civil justice, as defined by God's codified law, so that the image of God may be upheld in man (cf. Genesis 9:1-7).

Truly, the everyday life Adam and Eve first experienced in the Garden was intended to be transformed into godly culture that would honor the Lord, not to remain something for them to individually pursue in their own private relationship with Him. This image-of-God-oriented vision for all of life, built and managed under the righteous rule of the Almighty, is a far cry from the way the vast majority of twenty-first-century evangelicals think, particularly in the West. If we want to see change in our lands, with godliness the highest goal, we must return to this kind of creational mindset, thinking through and engaging cultural issues on God's terms instead of man's at each and every step along the way.

In the next chapter, I hope to clearly show the difference between moral law and positive law and how that was first demonstrated in the creational covenant. I also intend to reveal how the *covenant of works*, or *creational covenant* in Reformed thought, is contextualized in taking dominion, which is included in this covenant. In this way, I'll attempt to lay the groundwork for tracing the moral law through redemptive history so we can see how it applies to us today.

CHAPTER 2

THE ORIGINAL RELATIONSHIP BETWEEN GOD AND MAN

Have you ever wondered why people today should be blamed for what our first father Adam did? After all, he lived several thousands of years ago, right? Why should God count his sin against us? That doesn't seem fair. And how did he break God's law anyway? Wasn't he just forbidden from eating the fruit of one tree in the Garden? Eternal death for that offense seems more than overkill, doesn't it? I have heard many of these types of objections from unbelievers and sadly, the best that most Christians can offer is, "Well, we inherited our sin nature from Adam." While theologically true, such a pat answer doesn't actually interact with any of the concerns at hand. In order to appropriately respond, for our own benefit and for the benefit of others, we need to return to a robustly biblical understanding of covenant, particularly as it pertains to our first father, Adam.

WHAT ABOUT COVENANT?

The biblical concept of covenant is at the center of this discussion, stemming from the nature of God Himself. The Father, Son, and Holy Spirit have eternally been in covenant relationship and fellowship with One Another; Yahweh likewise determined to bend down to man, whom He created from the dust of the ground, and made a covenant relationship with him as well. The confession expresses it this way:

> Beside this law written in their hearts, they received a command not to eat of the tree of the knowledge of good and evil; which while they kept they were happy in their communion with God, and had dominion over the creatures (WCF, Ch. 4, Par.2).

We can see this in Genesis 2 where, upon creating man, God breathes life into his nostrils and places him in a special Garden within the eastern region of Eden. He then instructs him to work and keep it, forbidding him from eating from the tree of the knowledge of good and evil in the center of it. When Moses switches from referring to the Divine as "Elohim" in Chapter One to "Yahweh Elohim" in Chapter Two—"Yahweh" being His Self-given covenant name—he emphasizes the covenant relationship between God and Adam. Truly, the God of creation is Himself the God of the covenant!

So, what exactly is a covenant? In *Systematic Theology*, Louis Berkhof explains that the Hebrew word used for covenant is *berith* and is closely associated with *choq*, "an appointed statute or ordinance."[1] Thus, the *berith* that is established between Yahweh and man is an imposition from the greater to the lesser since the two are in no way equal. Both parties must fulfill certain requirements in order to maintain the relationship. Furthermore, the Hebrew word for love, *hesed*, is virtually synonymous with covenant faithfulness. For example, Psalm 89 is a psalm dealing heavily with God's covenant with David. Verse Two says, "For I said, 'Steadfast love will be built up forever; in the heavens you will establish your faithfulness.'" The psalmist purposely sets "steadfast love" in direct parallel with "faithfulness." Thus, the Hebraic concept of covenant involves the making and keeping of binding promises, together with specific stipulations, all within the context of an intimate relationship—one of a Father to a son.

This is the type of relationship Yahweh graciously imposed on Adam when He created him. But how do we actually know this to be the case, outside of hints in this direction within the text of Genesis 2? The simple answer is, "Because later Scripture explicitly says so." There are two key passages given under the inspiration of the Holy Spirit which help us properly understand the creational covenant: Hosea 6:7 and

---

[1] Louis Berkhof, *Systematic Theology*, Part 2: The Doctrine of Man In Relation to God: Man In the Covenant of Grace, https://systematictheology.us/p2s3c1.html.

Romans 5:12-21. These are not the only relevant texts but are certainly central to this discussion.

HOSEA 6:7

There are two contentions at play among those who would deny a prelapsarian (pre-fall) covenant divinely imposed on mankind. The first is that the Hebrew term *berith* nowhere appears within the first three chapters of Genesis. This argument suggests that such a covenant must be foisted upon the text from an extra-biblical theological framework, since the text itself does not explicitly tell us that the original relationship between God and man was covenantal in nature. The problem with this objection is that it completely ignores how later texts inform our understanding of those former. We have a direct parallel example to this situation. Nowhere in the text of 2 Samuel 7:4-7 do we find the word "covenant," even though this passage explains the details of God's covenant with King David concerning his Messianic descendant. Yet later, Psalm 89:3-4 speaks to promises contained in this passage and refers to it as a covenant. Psalm 89 makes explicit what was implicit in 2 Samuel 7. The same is true with Hosea 6:7 in relation to Genesis 2:16-17. In speaking to Israel's unfaithfulness to the covenant Yahweh made with her at Mount Sinai, Hosea draws a direct parallel with Adam's unfaithfulness to the covenant made with him in the Garden. The text reads, "But like Adam they transgressed the covenant; there they dealt faithlessly with me." Hosea 6 makes explicit what was implicit in Genesis 2. The harmony of God's Word is truly amazing!

The second objection seeks to nullify the above point by saying that the Hebrew word *adam* also means "mankind" in general and does not refer exclusively to our first father, Adam. Thus, Hosea 6:7 ought to read, "But like [mankind] they transgressed the covenant...." This would mean that the Noahic covenant is in view here, since it's the only other biblical covenant made with all of mankind. However, the parallel between mankind violating that covenant and Israel breaking her covenant would be quite strained at best, since the Noahic covenant concerns the general parameters for mankind as a whole living in God's world post-fall. Yet, the old covenant concerns specific requirements for a specific ethnic people living in a specific tract of land. The parallel made in Hosea 6:7 makes far more sense when Adam and his violation of the creational covenant are in view. Thus, there is no reason to move away from the way decent translations like the New American Standard Bible (NASB) and the English Standard Version (ESV) have rendered this verse.

ROMANS 5:12-21

In this section, the Apostle Paul builds on several key points discussed earlier in his epistle to the Romans. Among these are the universal and natural sinfulness of man, the utter futility of trying to gain peace with God through law-keeping, and man's absolute need to cling to Jesus' substitutionary atonement in His death in order for God to accept him into everlasting sonship with Him. This has been the apostle's teaching thus far in his epistle. He now makes it clear that it is only possible to belong to one of two humanities: one either finds himself naturally in Adam or, by a special act of grace, in Messiah Jesus. Thus, the concept of federal headship is introduced.

What is federal headship? "Federal" comes from the Latin term *foedus*, meaning "covenant." "Headship" speaks to the idea of representation. For instance, we can see this concept demonstrated when an employee damages someone else's property at a job site. In the eyes of the law, while the employee is at fault, it is the employer who's held responsible. Why? The employer represents the employee as his head before the law; therefore, being contractually joined, both the employer and the employee either own or fail to own that responsibility. This is what St. Paul is talking about, but within the redemptive-historical context of covenant.

The entire point of Romans 5:12ff finds its zenith in verses 18-19:

> Therefore, as one trespass led to condemnation for all men, so one
> act of righteousness leads to justification and life for all men. For
> as by the one man's disobedience the many were made sinners, so
> by the one man's obedience the many will be made righteous.

These two statements stand in parallel to each other and must be taken together. St. Paul's point is this: there are only two humanities to which someone can belong, on the basis of each humanity's respective covenantal representative. Because Adam is the federal head of all mankind under that first covenant, all men everywhere are at fault for their personal law-breaking and find themselves under the full weight of the curse of that covenant by virtue of being in Adam—this curse being death. This is why it's not enough to merely say that we're sinners by nature through our blood connection to our first father. No! Indeed, our natural bond to Adam is also covenantal. Jesus, unlike Adam, fully kept the creational covenant through His perfect obedience, and therefore all those in Him by faith alone also experience the full blessings promised in that covenant—this blessing being eternal life and glory. Our righteous standing with God the Father is not merely judicial by virtue of our faith in Messiah. No! Truly, our spiritual bond to Jesus is also covenantal.

WHAT ABOUT GOD'S LAW?

Now, this raises a vitally important question: "Since transgression is law-breaking, which law did Adam transgress and us in him?" Prior to Chapter Five in his epistle to the Romans, St. Paul explains that the content of God's moral standard broken by Jew and Gentile alike, whether internally imprinted or externally codified, is the same. He indicates that this law is summarized in the Ten Commandments (cf. Romans 2). The reason for this is that God is the law in and of Himself, and thus to be created in His likeness necessarily involves His righteous standards being written in our hearts.

Genesis 2:16-17 says, "And [Yahweh] God commanded the man, saying, 'You may surely eat of every tree of the garden, but of the tree of the knowledge of good and evil you shall not eat, for in the day that you eat of it you shall surely die.'" So, what then is the link between the law written in the heart and the specific command forbidding man from eating from the tree of the knowledge of good and evil? Are we to believe that Jesus, in obeying the rule which Adam broke, simply avoided one particular tree in eastern Israel during His entire earthly ministry, and thus procured His people's righteous standing with God? Such a simplistic reading of Genesis 2:16-17 and Romans 5:18-19 must be rejected as sub-biblical on its face. Instead, going back to John Calvin, Reformed theologians of all stripes have historically distinguished between *moral law* and *positive law*. *Moral law* refers to God's universal moral standard which stands unchanged for all time. This is the law which St. Paul spoke of in Romans 2. *Positive law*, on the other hand, is the application of the moral law within a particular covenant. In this case, Yahweh's command forbidding man to eat from the tree of the knowledge of good and evil was the positive law in the creational covenant. Indeed, Adam and Eve had no need whatsoever of discovering the difference between good and evil experientially since that knowledge had already been placed inside them as image bearers. This is precisely what Yahweh forbade and simultaneously what made Satan's words so tempting concerning eating the fruit of that tree. Thus, the essence of the creational covenant was, "If you perfectly, completely, and personally obey My law, you will gain the blessing of eternal life and glory. But, if you transgress it, you will gain the curse of death."

BRINGING THE PIECES TOGETHER

When Jesus kept the creational covenant in the place of all those He came to represent, He was obeying the moral law, which stood at the bottom of the prohibition specifically given to Adam in his covenantal and historical context. By doing this, He was acting as the true Image of God living in God's good world. He was living out the re-giving of the dominion mandate found in Genesis 9. If we want to know what it looks like to transform creation into culture that's built around the gospel of Jesus' kingdom rule, reclaiming the culture that's been built in rebellion against Him, we need to look at the totality of His life, death, and resurrection. We must also consider His current session, being seated at His Father's right hand. If we want to know what Adam failed to do as an image bearer in God's good creation—in stewarding, developing, and utilizing the rest of the created order on the principle of the moral law and its covenantal application—we must look to how Messiah fulfilled this role in His earthly ministry. We His redeemed followers must study and imitate our Master's example in light of what was expected of Adam before the fall, recognizing that we imperfectly do so. However, as the Spirit empowers us, we must live as the image bearers we're intended to be.

In the next chapter, I hope to introduce you to two giants of the Christian faith. These men, thinking in the biblical categories discussed above, sought to apply them within the context of a vision for every aspect of life coming under the rule of King Jesus, since His crown rights extend to the very ends of the earth. They self-consciously built on the Reformed and Puritan vision of Messiah's kingdom rule over all the nations. These leaders were in fact two Dutchmen, Abraham Kuyper and Cornelius Van Til. Let us now turn to a brief exploration of their work.

CHAPTER 3

MEET KUYPER AND VAN TIL: TWO GIANTS OF THE FAITH

INTRODUCING KUYPER

Abraham Kuyper is a prominent figure in Dutch history. He lived in the Netherlands from 1837 to 1920 and contributed greatly to the development of Reformed thought, both in theology and politics, as well as in society at large. For example, he was instrumental in establishing the Reformed Churches in the Netherlands *(Gereformeerde Kerken)*, which became the second largest Calvinistic confederation of local churches in his country. In addition, on the political front, Kuyper founded the Anti-Revolutionary Party and served as the Dutch Prime Minister between 1901 and 1905. Furthermore, Kuyper was involved in both national media and education. In this vein, he started a widespread newspaper, *De Standaard*, and founded a major university, Vrije Universiteit Amsterdam.[1] Arguably, his greatest contribution was his articulation of *sphere sovereignty*, a theological concept which under-girded all of these endeavors and more. Truly, the basis for this doctrine has its roots in John Calvin's exegetical and practical work, developed in the work of John Knox and the Covenanters in Scotland, and subsequently in that of the seventeenth- and eighteenth-century English Puritans. Indeed, Kuyper was very much standing on the shoulders of those who preceded him in developing and applying the doctrine of *sphere sovereignty* further.

The essence of Kuyperian thought can rightly be boiled down to "if not Christ, then chaos." This is also the essence of Van Til's contribution to Reformed thought, which will be discussed below. Colossians 1:15-20 reveals that nothing exists except that which Jesus has created, sustains, and carries along to its intended end. Not only this, but Jesus Himself asserted His universal authority over all things as God's Messianic King when He said, "All authority in heaven and on earth has been given to me" (Matthew 28:18). Now, where exactly does He say He has "all authority"? Not only in heavenly, spiritual matters, but also in earthly, temporal matters. When did He receive this authority? In His resurrected glory, since He says it "has [already] been given to me," and this

---

[1] Britannica, *Abraham Kuyper: Dutch Theologian and Statesman*, https://www.britannica.com/biography/Abraham-Kuyper.

being said after His resurrection and just prior to His ascension. Therefore, not only as Creator, but also as Messianic King, does Jesus have crown rights over every square millimeter whereby He rightfully declares, "Mine! Mine! Mine!"[2]

Holy Scripture identifies three main spheres of limited authority in society which are subject directly to King Jesus and His unlimited Messianic authority, since it was He Who instituted them in the first place. These are: (1) the family, (2) the congregation, and (3) the state. While these spheres may occasionally overlap, each remains a distinct and separate societal arena of authority, with its own God-prescribed purpose, structure, responsibilities, and extent of authority. Indeed, all three of these jurisdictions presuppose the self-governance of the individuals who compose them. To the individual, God has given the full extent of finite governance, but over only one person, namely, himself—thus, what the Bible calls "self-control" or "self-governance." To the family, the Lord has granted parents an extensive amount of authority over a small group of people. Likewise, to the congregation, Jesus has delegated elder-pastors a medium amount of authority over a medium-sized group of people. Finally, He's delegated to the civil governing authorities a highly limited extent of authority over a very large group of people. Each of these spheres will be explored in upcoming chapters. For now what is clear is that, as an intrinsically orderly God, Messiah Jesus has a specific way He

---

[2] Greg L. Bahnsen, *By This Standard*, Kindle Location 52.

desires society as a whole to be organized and to function, being directly under His kingdom rule.

INTRODUCING VAN TIL

Cornelius Van Til lived from 1895 to 1987. He spent the first ten years of his life in the Netherlands, but then he immigrated with his family to Indiana, USA. He taught at Princeton University, but after a time left with a group of conservative teachers from the school to found Westminster Theological Seminary in order to defend and uphold both the inerrancy of Scripture, and the historic Reformed and evangelical faith. This group included J. Gresham Machen, Westminster's first president. This was during the time of B.B. Warfield, who remained behind at Princeton to continue the battle against the increasing encroachment of theological liberalism. Van Til is known for his work in theologically derived philosophy, particularly on the point of *presuppositional apologetics*. However, this presuppositional approach to apologetics and gospel preaching soon grew legs and walked right out into the public square to address the unbelieving culture.[3]

So, what is the presuppositional approach? Van Til developed this approach to apologetics—that is, the defense of the Christian faith—by building on three fundamental truths revealed in God's Word. The first is the formal principle of the Reformation, *Sola Scriptura*. This doctrine asserts that the sixty-six-book corpus of God's holy, inspired, and

---

[3] Theopedia, *Cornelius Van Til*, https://www.theopedia.com/cornelius-van-til.

unalterable Word is the sole infallible rule for all of faith and practice. Therefore, Scripture is entirely sufficient, perspicuous, authoritative, and necessary in all it teaches. The clearest place where this is taught, and most forcefully, is at 2 Timothy 3:16-17 which says, "All Scripture is breathed out by God and profitable for teaching, for reproof, for correction, and for training in righteousness, that the man of God may be complete, equipped for every good work." Thus, Van Til insisted that Holy Scripture is the only proper grounds of authority on which a Christian must stand and from which he must make his arguments for the truth.

Secondly, Van Til picked up on St. Paul's teaching to the Colossians, which expresses that not only is Jesus preeminent in every matter as the Creator and Sustainer of all things (cf. Colossians 1:15-20), but He is also the principium of all true wisdom and knowledge wherever it may be found. Colossians 2:3 teaches of Messiah Jesus, "in whom are hidden all the treasures of wisdom and knowledge." Furthermore, elsewhere the apostle teaches that He is "the power of God and the wisdom of God" (1 Corinthians 1:24). This means that Jesus Himself is the one and only reference point for truly knowing anything about anything, since He is the principle from which all of it flows. How do we come to know what He defines as reality, and have the proper categories to interpret it and live thereby, save in His most holy Word? In this way, Van Til concluded that any extra-biblical evidences we discover to be true only serve to confirm and bolster what Yahweh has already said in His Word—not the other way round, as many suppose. Why? Christ Jesus and His law-Word is the ultimate level of knowledge and authority—the highest court of appeal, as it were—and therefore all other sources of knowledge and authority must bow the knee in conformity to His inscripturated revelation. In this way, this second truth is inseparably linked together with the first.

Finally, Van Til insisted on the basis of Scripture that neither Yahweh nor His moral (unchanging) law need to be proven to the unbeliever, since these things are self-evident to all men, regardless of location or upbringing. Appealing to these self-evident truths is not the same as seeking to prove them. Romans 1:18ff makes it clear that mankind, each and every one, is naturally in a state of actively suppressing the truth of God in his willful unrighteousness. How? Even though Yahweh has made Himself plainly known through His created order, sinners insist upon exchanging the truth of Who the immortal Creator actually is for something of their own liking, something from creation. St. Paul gives sodomy as his chief example, then follows this up with a list of vices, to demonstrate how this rebellion plays out in everyday life. The apostle concludes this by saying, "Though they know God's righteous decree that those who practice such things deserve to die, they not only do them but give approval to those who practice them" (vs. 32). The apostle Paul explains to the Romans in Chapter Two that even Gentiles, who did not receive the law as did the Jews, are still accountable to God for breaking it, since the sum and substance of it has also been written on their hearts as His image bearers (cf. Romans 2:14-15). In this way, Van Til argued that when speaking with the unbeliever, a Christian must never lose sight of the truth that his neighbor is also made in the image of God and therefore intuitively knows the truth of his Creator's existence. This is the moral standard by which he will be judged, and he naturally suppresses these things in hot rebellion day and night. Thus, the apologist's twofold task, with the goal of presenting the gospel of grace in a meaningful way, becomes that of Proverbs 26:4-5, "Answer not a fool according to his folly, lest you be like him yourself. Answer a fool according to his folly, lest he be wise in his own eyes." This means we must avoid at all costs moving away from Scripture as our grounds of authority to some sort of "neutral" middle ground. At the same time, we must seek to help the sinner with whom we speak to see the folly of his own position via an internal critique at a foundational level.[4]

KUYPER, VAN TIL, AND ETHICS

So, how does Cornelius Van Til's Scripturally derived presuppositional way of thinking apply to the issue of ethics and, subsequently, how does that relate to Abraham Kuyper's doctrine of sphere sovereignty? Indeed, Van Til's fundamental framework for thinking through the ethical implications of *Presuppositionalism* was Kuyper's work on *sphere sovereignty*. So, the question is, "When we speak of the social arena of family, how do we know the way that particular government is meant to function? By what standard should it do so? And who says so?" What about for the individual? What about for the state? What about for the local church? In

---

[4] See Cornelius Van Til, *The Defense of the Faith*, Philadelphia, PA: P&R Publishing, 2008.

paraphrasing Jesus, Van Til would insist, "There is no neutrality!" (cf. Mark 9:40). Therefore, the question is never *whether* there's an ultimate authority that's calling the shots and being served, but *which* one. Likewise, it's never *whether* there's a governing moral standard in any given social sphere, but *which* one.[5] As Van Til would say, there are really only two options: *theonomy* (God's law) or *autonomy* (man's law).[6] Together with the rest of historic Reformed orthodoxy—whether they be Scottish Covenanters, English Puritans, or French Huguenots—both Kuyper and Van Til would insist that the only ultimate authority is King Jesus and the only ultimate standard by which He governs the world is His good, eternal, and immutable law. The summary of this moral law is contained in the Ten Commandments, and its general equity (principle) is found in those positive (circumstantial) laws which apply the Decalogue to various and sundry situations, as given in their covenantal contexts across Holy Writ.

Most importantly, the underlying assumptions throughout this entire paradigm are that: (1) Jesus is the ultimate Ruler of kings on earth, (2) all men must obey Him in their specific stations of life and social arenas, and must do so in accordance with the totality of His law-Word, and (3) no one is capable of doing so from the heart, in a way that's actually acceptable to God, apart from the Spirit's supernatural work of

---

[5] See Rousas J. Rushdoony, *The Institutes of Biblical Law*, Philadelphia, PA: P&R Publishing, 1973.
[6] See Cornelius Van Til, *In Defense of Biblical Christianity*, Vol. 3: Christian Theistic Ethics, Philadelphia, PA: P&R Publishing, 1970, p. 134.

regeneration. A new heart always precedes and results in a new life lived under the Lordship of Christ.

In the next several chapters, I hope to build upon this paradigm of social authority and ethics in all four spheres: the individual, the family, the local church, and the state. I believe that it's vitally important for us as followers of Christ to understand both the framework and responsibilities of any given sphere, and how that sphere is meant to interact with the others, since they are all subservient to the rule of King Jesus Himself.

CHAPTER 4

SELF-GOVERNANCE

In our current cultural milieu in the West, when the average person hears of "self-governance," he or she automatically fills in the definition with "self-actualization." Thus, the *individual* is most important. "It's my life, so I can determine my own destiny!" "It's my body, so it's my choice!" "I can determine for myself what is right and wrong!" The words of Ernest Henley have become the mantra of the modern man: "I am the master of my fate: I am the captain of my soul." Now, the question lurking beneath the surface would be, "Is this view of self-governance actually true? And how can we truly know?"

EXPOSING THE FOOL'S FOLLY

Proverbs 26:5 says, "Answer the fool according to his folly, lest he be wise in his own eyes." Who is the morally foolish one, save the unbeliever who insists on suppressing the truth of God in unrighteousness? So, let's put this view to the test. If it's the truth of the matter, then it will be internally coherent and consistent. As Dr. James White often points out, "Inconsistency is the sign of a failed argument."[1] So, what happens when we try to push this philosophy of self-actualization out into the corners of life? What we find is that although it initially creates a sense of self-worth and personal responsibility, over the long-term it proves to be untenable, since no one individual actually possesses the power to actualize his own self-made reality. Such a perspective on life leads the modern man to look to societal bodies who appear to have great power and resources in order to accomplish this vision. Some look to God and the local church to make this happen. Some look to spirits on a parallel plane to gain such power. Some look to the strong arm of the civil governing authorities. However, in each case, the individual is "bending over backwards" to use one of these avenues as a means to an end—that end being his or her own self-actualization. The very fact that the one imagining his own destiny cannot actually bring it about in real life is itself a self-refutation—it

---

[1] Shabir Ally, *The Distinction Between an Inconsistent Person and an Inconsistent Argument*, https://answeringmissionaries.wordpress.com/2006/05/25/the-distinction-between-an-inconsistent-person-and-an-inconsistent-argument/. Anthony Fava, *Jeff Durbin, James White Own Brandan Robertson In Debate On Homosexuality*, https://evangelicaldarkweb.org/2023/03/11/jeff-durbin-james-white-own-brandan-robertson-in-debate/.

demonstrates that this perspective on life and the world cannot stand up under its own weight and is therefore spiritual folly.

YAHWEH HAS SPOKEN

In Chapter One, I explained how God's law is the expression of His own moral character, how all men everywhere intuitively know His law as being created in His likeness, and how the summation of that law has been codified in the Ten Commandments. This means that the *imago Dei* (image of God) is at the heart of God's law and how He defines His terms therein.

God's law always treats the individual as a personally culpable being living in community with others, not the other way round. This means that the individual is more essential than the group, which is the exact opposite of what men like Marx, Marcuse, and Kendi have written. This principle is made explicit at Deuteronomy 24:16, "Fathers shall not be put to death because of their children, nor shall children be put to death because of their fathers. Each one shall be put to death for his own sin."

As a point of application, Deuteronomy 24:16 exposes the unlawfulness of the argument that says abortion is acceptable in the case of rape—the father ought to be justly put to death by the state for the crime of rape, not his unborn child. Now, how do we know the death penalty is due for rape? Because Jesus says so. Deuteronomy 22:25-27 instructs, "But if in the open country a man meets a young woman who is betrothed, and the man seizes her and lies with her, then only the man who lay with her shall die. But you shall do nothing to the young woman; she has committed no offense punishable by death. For this case is like that of a man attacking and murdering his neighbor, because he met her in the open country, and though the betrothed young woman cried for help there was no one to rescue her." Notice the parties that are personally responsible here: (1) the man is culpable before the law for committing the crime of rape, (2) the young lady is responsible for crying out for help as the victim (cp. Deuteronomy 22:23-24), (3) the civil judges are responsible for impartially and hastily bringing justice on the guilty out of love for the victim (cf. Leviticus 19:15), and (4) any passerby is expected to personally intervene in the situation, so as to rescue the victim from harm. This means that self-governance, as driven by love for God and love for neighbor, is first and foremost a resolute mindset that says, "I will gladly obey the Lord my God no matter what it may cost me in the process." This is a part of the OT background St. Paul seems to have in mind when he pens, "But the fruit of the Spirit is…self-control; against such things there is no law" (Galatians 5:22-23). The reason "there is no law" against self-control is that the Triune God's good and holy law is all about self-governance, as given within the context of individuals being His image bearers, who are personally accountable for their desires, thoughts, words, and actions. Indeed, self-control is a very active, intentional thing for which each and every one is individually culpable ultimately to King Jesus' divine court.

Now, let's shift to the other aspect of biblical self-governance. Within the context of discussing "clean" versus "unclean," Yahweh commands His people on the basis of Who He is, saying, "Consecrate yourselves therefore, and be holy, for I am holy" (Leviticus 11:44). What does it mean to be "holy"? Contained within this biblical term are both the aspects of moral purity and separation. As the transcendent, eternal Being that He is, Yahweh is both infinitely pure and infinitely separate from His creation. Thus, He instructs His image bearers to imitate Him on the creaturely level. The point of all the clean/unclean laws under the old covenant was to teach the children of Israel to live in a distinct, counter-cultural way over and against the pagan nations around them. Why? Because they belonged to Yahweh, not the Baals, and therefore all their cultural activity and development was meant to reflect that basic truth. This means that the dietary laws of Deuteronomy 14 were not about protecting an ancient civilization from health risks, but rather about drawing a clear line of delineation between Yahweh's people and those idolatrous peoples around her. Moses explicitly says this in his preamble to these laws, "For you are a people holy to [Yahweh] your God, and [Yahweh] has chosen you to be a people for his treasured possession, out of all the peoples who are on the face of the earth" (Deuteronomy 14:2).

Indeed, the Newer Testament picks up this principle and applies it to the new covenant people of Messiah Jesus. St. James writes, "Religion that is pure and undefiled before God, the Father, is this: to visit orphans and widows in their affliction, and to keep oneself unstained from the world" (James 1:27). The apostle Paul expresses it like this, "Do not be unequally yoked with unbelievers. For what partnership has righteousness with lawlessness? Or what fellowship has light with darkness? What accord has Christ with Belial? Or what portion does a believer share with an unbeliever? What agreement has the temple of God with idols?" (2 Corinthians 6:14-16). This may apply to such intimate partnerships as covenanting together in marriage, entering together into business endeavours, forming a political party, or preparing to preach the Gospel at an abortion mill. The fundamental question here must always be, "By what standard shall we do such and such? And, who says so?" Without being on the same page at this foundational level, as defined by God's unalterable Word, even ostensible Christians may find themselves in a kind of partnership with one another that's unholy, unequally yoked, and superficially unified at best. This also seems to be a part of what St. Paul is referring to when he teaches by the moving of the Holy Spirit, "But the fruit of the Spirit is…self-control" (Galatians 5:22-23). Again, self-governance is biblically a very active, intentional thing for which each individual is ultimately responsible to the Lord Jesus, the Judge of all the earth Who always does what is right.

While the real-life applications to the doctrine of self-governance are myriad, what I have outlined above is the sum and substance of what the Triune God says about this particular sphere of creaturely sovereignty. Self-control means pursuing glad obedience to King Jesus, as defined by His law-Word, no matter the cost involved. It likewise means pursuing separateness from the world via exclusively entering "equally yoked" close partnerships.

It's important to remember in all of this that because Yahweh has spoken, this is the reality of the situation, the way things actually are.

Thus, to attempt to live contrary to reality is both rebellion and insanity. It is rebellion because God has created us in His image to live in His good world in a particular way, and it is insanity because for one to be convinced in his heart and mind that he must continually try to live by some kind of alternate reality instead of what's objectively true, is by definition insane.[2] Where some mental illnesses may be induced by chemical imbalances, this sort of mental illness is wholly and intentionally self-induced by a heart that hates the light of God's Self-revelation throughout nature and Holy Writ. The only proper remedy to this moral condition is the kind of repentance before a most holy and merciful God found in Psalm 51. This sort of repentance is personal, total, and heartfelt. Truly, "the sacrifices of God are a broken spirit; a broken and contrite heart, O God, you will not despise" (Psalm 51:17). The answer to sin must always be, "Kiss"—loyally obey—"the Son, lest he be angry, and you perish in the way, for his wrath is quickly kindled. Blessed are all who take refuge in him" (Psalm 2:12).

In the next chapter, I hope to explore the familial government. This government is the first social institution God established as part of His created order, which as we will see is the foundational building block of society.

---

[2] Cambridge Dictionary, *Insanity*, https://dictionary.cambridge.org/dictionary/english/insanity.

CHAPTER 5

FAMILY: THE FIRST GOVERNMENT IN SOCIETY UNDER GOD

Determining which group is the foundational building block of society is a vitally important issue. One might ask, "Who is most integral to a society or nation—the individual, family, church, or state?" How we answer this question will determine what we are most committed to protecting as a society. Whichever conclusion we come to will determine the party against whom treason has been committed—treason being the highest form of betrayal in society, deserving of the most severe judicial penalty. In the West today we have two competing views. On the one hand, many have been trained by secular humanism to think that the autonomous, self-actualizing individual is the most fundamental component of society, and therefore those opposing the individual are guilty of treason. We can see this in the way many pro-choice advocates respond to the truth that abortion is the unjustified taking of human life in the womb. When presented with the fact that the mother is guilty of infanticide by intentionally hiring an assassin in a lab coat, and that forgiveness for this terrible sin exists and can be found only in Jesus Christ, their responses are utterly volatile.[1] On the other hand, many have been convinced of cultural Marxist ideology, which treats the all-powerful state as the most integral unit in a given society. In those cases, treason is always against the state, that is, the civil governing authorities of a nation. We can see this in how Former Prime Minister Trudeau and his Liberal government responded by declaring martial law in Canada's national capital in response to a peaceful protest against a public policy issue (February 2022).[2]

Are either of these views actually true? Are they able to remain internally consistent when subjected to the scrutiny of cross-examination? Let us pursue this subject more closely.

---

[1] For an example of this, see Apologia Studios, "Warning: Salt Lake Showdown," https://youtu.be/GGPkZ9t46c4.

[2] See Jordan B. Peterson, "The Catastrophe of Canada | Rex Murphy and Jordan B Peterson," https://youtu.be/5efyUt5YDU0.

CRITIQUING THE "INDIVIDUAL" VIEW

Is the individual important in society? Absolutely. I demonstrated this truth in the previous chapter. However, people don't live as isolated individuals, floating through life in impenetrable bubbles. We most naturally exist within the context of relationship with each other; even the few hermits living in the backwoods of Siberia still have parents, siblings, and neighbors, albeit living miles apart from one another. Trying to live as isolated individuals only results in the breakdown of society, not the flourishing of it. Truly, man was created for the lifelong covenantal relationship of marriage, in order that he and his wife would be "fruitful and multiply and fill the earth and subdue it" (Gen. 1:28), turning creation into a God-glorifying culture. It's impossible to do any part of this alone. Thus, this vision for the self-actualization of autonomous, modern man is once again shown to be the self-refuting, incoherent perspective on life that it is.

CRITIQUING THE "STATE" VIEW

Many in our Western countries have also bought into the cultural Marxist's worldview. They have become convinced of the delusion that somehow, in joining these revolutionaries in fighting against every manner of alleged societal injustice, and in looking to the long arm of the state to forcefully fix these injustices, they will achieve their dreams of self-actualization. The problem of course is that Marxism—no matter its permutation—is fundamentally a statist philosophy, meaning the state seeks to absorb all spheres and arenas of life into itself so it can micromanage society across the board. The goal is to bring about equality of outcome for all groups, calling it "equity." This is fundamentally at odds with the individual's aspirations of actualizing their own reality. This has also been proven eight or nine times throughout history to be absolutely detrimental to human flourishing and the development of society as a whole, since it serves to fundamentally crush its citizens to the level of slavery—captivity to the will of the civil government, that is. For example, we have seen this play out in such countries as the former Soviet Union, China, Cuba, Venezuela, and North Korea where the state has oppressed and murdered millions of its own citizens.[3] Thus, this statist worldview can be seen to be self-defeating, since it can never build anything, but can only destroy.

CRITIQUING SACRALISM

Since we have now established that it's neither the individual nor the state that's most integral to society, we are left with the church and the family as our options. Medieval Europe operated on the notion that the institutional church equalled the kingdom of God and therefore was most integral to society. In the medieval Roman Catholic view, the civil government possessed the power of the sword to order the earthly kingdom (civil society) back into the heavenly kingdom, which was found in the institutional church. At the same time, the church held the power of per-

---

[3] For an accurate depiction of the Marxist strategy implemented in these and other countries, see George Orwell, *Nineteen Eighty-Four*, London: Penguin UK, 2008.

suasion, seeking to add heavenly goods to the natural goods found in the earthly kingdom in order to complete them and Christianize them. Essentially, the state was free to punish those who did not conform to the official teaching and practice of the church. This resulted in little difference between civil and ecclesial due process. In this way, in practice everything in European society slowly came under the direct control of the Roman Catholic Church and her Papacy. Indeed, she went far beyond her role in rightly preaching the Word to God's people, rightly administering unto them the sacraments of Holy Communion and baptism, and rightly following ecclesial due process in administering church discipline.

As the apostle Paul instructed his young protégé Timothy, the primary function of the local church is discipleship: "I charge you in the presence of God and of Christ Jesus, who is to judge the living and the dead, and by his appearing and his kingdom: preach the word; be ready in season and out of season; reprove, rebuke, and exhort, with complete patience and teaching" (2 Timothy 4:1-2). Additionally, the local church only secondarily facilitates the care of physical needs between believers (cf. Acts 6:1-7). In contrast, Rome created a hierarchy over and above individual local congregations and regional church councils, and the Pope was treated as a king who had the authority to govern everything from regional economics to international conquests through the state. This constitutes an absolute abuse of God-given ecclesial authority—it's spiritual abuse in the extreme.

FAMILY AS GOVERNMENT

Now that I have demonstrated the impossibility of the contrary, allow me to set forth God's answer regarding which social sphere is the true foundational building block of society, and do so standing firmly on His holy Word. To begin with, we can see in Genesis 2 that Yahweh Himself instituted the family as the first government in society. This government has both a creational role, as well as a typological role; it's designed to both turn creation into culture as God's image bearers live in His good world, as well as typify Christ's covenantal relationship with His blood-bought Bride, the Church.

Furthermore, we can see how the law itself treats the family as the foundational building block of society. How so? The crime of treason is reserved for undermining and betraying God's intended family governmental structure and purpose. We know this by the severity of the penal sanctions He requires for doing so. There are three situations where the image of God has been so attacked in an individual that the only way of legally upholding the value of that person is through the death penalty—murder, rape and sexual abuse, and kidnapping. Yet, the death penalty is not required for the sins of going against self-, civil, or church government. However, it is in the case with the institution of family. God's good and holy law is clear: adultery, incest, sodomy, and bestiality all deserve the death penalty. Why? "Their blood is upon them" (cf. Leviticus 20:10-16). Thus, through civil due process, as outlined in Deuteronomy 19:15-21, the civil government must try, convict, and punish individuals convicted of these particular crimes with public execution. This is how much God values the family as the foundational building block of society in His good and just social order.

Now, for many a committed Christian in the twenty-first century, this runs hard against their modern sensibilities. First, it seems very backward. Second, it seems harsh. And third, it seems to contradict the notion that, since we're now under the new covenant, we're under grace, not the law. To the first objection, I would humbly and respectfully point out that trying to argue that what came before is morally inferior to where we are now as an advanced people is a case of "chronological snobbery"—it's a logical fallacy because it fails to meaningfully interact with the substance of the argument. To the second, this is an argument from subjective preference—"I reject this because I find it icky." Again, appealing to personal preferences fails to provide a meaningful response. Lastly, rejecting the Newer Testament's usage of Older Testament ethical imperatives on the basis of "we're under grace, rather than the law" is an error in hermeneutics, since it fails to follow Scripture's own interpretative methodology, namely, that later revelation interprets, explains, and applies former revelation. Therefore, we're not allowed to cut the message of the Bible into tiny bits and so undermine its intrinsic unity. It seems that all three of these objections are attempts to justify a deep emotional revulsion to the idea that God's law, when properly understood on the Bible's own terms, is meant to be applied in its totality to every group of people in every age, including our modern context. However, this type of reasoning fails to interact meaningfully with the substance of God's law, including the aspects concerning treason against the family government. Nor does it take into consideration Who the Bible says is its source, namely the Lord of glory.

So, why do I believe that we can know with certainty that the family is the foundational building block of society? How can we know with certainty that treason is against the societal government of family and rightly deserves the death penalty? How do we know that this is God's unchanging ethical standard for all men in all places at all times? We can know these things because the Triune God of Holy Scripture says so. Leviticus 20:10-16 plainly identifies adultery, incest, sodomy, and bestiality, not only as sins which require the guilty one's repentance before God and their fellow man, but also as crimes deserving of a quick, humane, and state-enacted execution. Which God-ordained institution do all four of these crimes directly attack and undermine? They attack the jurisdiction of the family. Are these statutes genuinely a good thing and, if so, on what basis can we say this? This is the psalmist's God-inspired response to this question: "You are good and do good; teach me your statute...the law of your mouth is better to me than thousands of gold and silver pieces" (Psalm 119:68, 72). Furthermore, how do we know that these statutes are actually righteous and just in and of themselves, and therefore are required today? Again, David wrote by the moving of the Holy Spirit, "The heavens are yours; the earth also is yours; the world and all that is in it, you have founded them" and "Righteousness and justice are the foundation of your throne; steadfast love and faithfulness go before you" (Psalm 89:11, 14). God's law is intrinsically good, righteous, and just because it's the codification of God's own character, which is itself absolutely good, righteous, and just. Therefore, it's a very dangerous thing indeed to reject any of the requirements of God's law because to do so fundamentally constitutes a rejection of His very character. In this way, the law teaches us that the family government is God's foundational building block in society, in addition to that which was given in Genesis Chapter Two.

As I explained in Chapter Three, the above biblical categories formed the entire basis for Kuyper and Van Til's theological and philosophical thought process. This was not unique to them but found its expression in Reformed thought stretching back to the Reformation. Indeed, John Calvin spoke often of the "three uses of the law"—that God's law is useful for showing unbelievers their rebellion, for teaching believers how to grow in godliness, and for the establishment of an orderly society under King Jesus. In the next two chapters, I hope to continue building on this fertile ground in examining the governments of church and state, as well as how they are meant to relate to one another.

CHAPTER 6

SINS VERSUS CRIMES

The distinction between "sins" and "sins that are also crimes" is a biblical distinction that touches all of us. For example, does God view some sins as worse than others? Does Jesus hold a distinction between church and state and, if so, on what basis? If such a separation exists in His economy, who is responsible for dealing with unrepentant sin at a heart level and who is responsible for dealing with crime at a behavioral level? Does this mean that King Jesus is just as concerned with justice in society as He is with mercy? Does His Messianic authority extend even to the civil magistrate in how he rules? These are vitally important questions for every follower of Christ to sort through.

HOW DO WE KNOW?

Long ago in the days of Noah, when God republished His creational covenant with mankind, He established the judicial principle of *lex talionis*, that is, the "law of exact retributive justice." Genesis 9:5-6 teaches, "And for your lifeblood I will require a reckoning: from every beast I will require it and from man. From his fellow man I will require a reckoning for the life of man. Whoever sheds the blood of man, by man shall his blood be shed, for God made man in his own image." It's important to recognize that *lex talionis* was established as part and parcel of the dominion mandate, a covenantal requirement for all men everywhere at all times, which was established *prior* to the old covenant. For a Christian to run away from this truth would amount to him attempting to escape being created in God's very likeness!

Now, this principle of justice is later expressed throughout the law of Moses as "life for life, eye for eye, tooth for tooth, hand for hand, foot for foot, burn for burn, wound for wound, stripe for stripe" (Exodus 21:23-25). This principle is applied in various ways, including paying back double for thefts (cf. Exodus 22:4) and using equal weights and measures in business (cf. Deuteronomy 25:13-16). At the heart of *lex talionis* is upholding the image of God, which is why Deuteronomy 19 teaches the presumption of innocence in civil investigations and court proceedings. We can see this principle applied elsewhere in Older Testament law, as well. For example, we see that health is presumed until physical evidences are established by a trained medical practitioner (cf.

Leviticus 13). And later, in the Newer Testament, we see this in the presumption of innocence of a church member or leader until two to three lines of witness and testimony are established by a plurality of ecclesiastical judges (elder-pastors) (cf. 1 Timothy 5:19). However, what the law makes abundantly clear in Deuteronomy 19:21 is that Yahweh's administrator of civil justice is exclusively the civil governing authorities—neither parents, nor elder-pastors, nor other ordinary citizens are permitted to arbitrarily take this role upon themselves.

We can see this distinction between sins and crimes most clearly in Deuteronomy 22:8 which says, "When you build a new house, you shall make a parapet for your roof, that you may not bring the guilt of blood upon your house, if anyone should fall from it." The principle here is that love for neighbor demands being concerned for his physical welfare beforehand. Notice this is meant to prevent "bring[ing] the guilt of blood upon your house." This means there hasn't yet been any physical harm done to either one's neighbor or his property. Due to the presumption of innocence in God's law, there's no penal sanction attached to this law. While violating this command would indeed constitute *sin* requiring repentance, it doesn't qualify as a *crime*. Why? There's no penal sanction by which the civil magistrate may enforce this as civil law. Now, if the homeowner decided to neglect constructing a railing or wall around the perimeter of his ancient flat rooftop and then one of his friends or family members fell off his roof to their peril, then he would be deserving of a proper trial and, a panel of judges establishing his guilt, the due penalty against him would be enacted (cf. Deuteronomy 19:15-21).

The following represents the way that things are supposed to work in a just society, where both legislators and law enforcement are believers seeking to live under the rule of King Jesus themselves, as well as to influence those who do not. Allow me to provide some modern-day examples for consideration:

1. A family has built an in-ground swimming pool for recreational purposes. Love for neighbor would require building a fence around the pool so that someone walking by may not fall in. If, for whatever reason, the family doesn't think it necessary to take such precautions, while it would certainly be sin, it would not be a crime in God's eyes, since no harm has yet taken place. However, the minute that someone trips and drowns in the pool, a crime has taken place, which must be answered by the civil magistrate with God's prescribed penalty.

2. A roadworks crew has set up alongside a road. Love for neighbor would require setting up a perimeter of blockades and warning signs to keep drivers and pedestrians alike from entering the work zone where they may get injured. Failing to set up the perimeter by itself would be sin, according to God's law. Failing to do so and resulting in the injury of a neighbor entering the work zone would be a crime. While the industry's best practices may indeed *recommend* setting up a work zone perimeter, the state cannot lawfully *enforce* this recommendation. It is only when actual harm has been committed against one's neighbor that the due penalty for that specific act of harm may be enforced by the state—upon the completion of the required due process, that is.

3. Finally, we currently have two different types of speed limit signs in Canada: *regulatory signs* that are white with black edging and

warning signs that are yellow with black bordering. The former indicates the government-set speed limit, financial penalties for violations, and that police officers have the authority to enforce it, while the latter indicates a strong recommendation of a safe speed limit, no penalties for violations, and that officers have no authority to enforce it. In our currently unjust society, regulatory speed limit signs represent a presumption of guilt prior to any harm being committed against one's neighbor or his property, while warning speed limit signs serve the same purpose as a fence around a pool or a barricade and signage around a work zone. The former is unlawful in God's eyes, while the latter is lawful. This means the state, in cooperation with those constructing the road, ought to replace all regulatory speed signs with warning signs.

ANALOGIA FIDE HARD AT WORK

During the Reformation, a crucial point of hermeneutics was rediscovered, namely, *analogia fide (the analogy of faith)*. This means that in order to properly interpret any single passage of Scripture, we must keep the entire story of God's work in history in mind—from creation, to the fall, to the redemption of all things in Christ, to their final restoration and completion on the Last Day. A necessary aspect of this redemptive-historical principle of interpretation is the principle that later revelation is given to properly explain and apply former revelation. In this way, we're constrained to think God's thoughts after Him as His Word interprets itself.

So how do Jesus and His apostles explain and apply Older Testament ethical imperatives? Do they uphold this distinction in the law between "sins" and "sins that are also crimes"? The place to turn to answer this question is Jesus' Sermon on the Mount, which Matthew records for us in his Gospel account in Matthew 5-7. Herein, our Lord explicitly states that He came not "to abolish" any of the OT ethical imperatives, but rather "to fulfill them" through perfectly keeping them (Matthew 5:17)—this is the exact opposite stance to that of many evangelicals today, who view Older Testament ethics as having little to no bearing on our lives today. Jesus goes on to say that obedience to the law is not optional for those who wish to follow Him under His kingdom rule—and this obedience must begin in the heart and work its way out into action—unlike the external-only pseudo-obedience of the conservative Jewish leadership of His day (Matthew 5:17-20). In addition, the righteousness of citizens in His kingdom must "*exceed* that of the scribes and Pharisees" (emphasis added) by operating exclusively on the principle of *Sola Scriptura (Only Scripture)*—their sole moral standard must be God's law-Word, not a combination of Scripture and the Jewish oral tradition, which would later be called the *Mishnah*.[1]

Jesus goes on to explain, through providing six antitheses, how the tires of His kingdom's ethical standard meet the pavement of everyday life. The section of application that's most directly relevant to our discussion here is found in Matthew 5:38-42. Our Master begins, "You have heard that it was said, 'An eye for eye and a tooth for tooth.'" While this could legitimately be a reference back to either Exodus 21:24 or

---

[1] See Joseph Boot, *The Mission of God: A Manifesto of Hope for Society*, Toronto: Ezra Press, 2016, p. 96-98. Dr. Boot provides an excellent summary of Christ's view of the law in this section.

Leviticus 24:20, considering what follows, it makes more sense that Jesus is intentionally quoting from Deuteronomy 19:21. The context here is God's design for the civil due process of investigation and conviction of crime. Now, some have surmised that Jesus is replacing the law of Moses with His own superior law, the law of love. However, this cannot be since our Lord began this section of teaching by upholding the unchanging substance of Older Testament ethics in their entirety (cf. Matthew 5:17-20). Instead, the Messiah is here contrasting what the law actually says, which He Himself gave, with the Jewish leaders' abuse of it. How were they doing this? Through the Mishnah-informed, external-only kind of religion they had created.

Jesus continues, "But I say to you, Do not resist the one who is evil. But if anyone slaps you on the right cheek, turn to him the other also. And if anyone would sue you and take your tunic, let him have your cloak as well. And if anyone forces you to go one mile, go with him two miles. Give to the one who begs from you, and do not refuse the one who would borrow from you" (Matthew 5:39-42). Here, Messiah is pitting pure religion—one that requires wholehearted obedience to God's revealed Word, as the sole infallible rule of doctrine and practice—against the scribes and Pharisees' mangled, false religion. How were they practicing a mangled, false religion? First, they were attempting to operate both by God's Word and by their ancient oral tradition, which inevitably led to them making the former subservient to the latter (cf. Matthew 15:1-9). As a result, they attempted to act as civil magistrates in bringing penal sanctions against their neighbors without properly following civil due process or actually being civil magistrates. We can see this in the first example given—Jesus says, "Do not resist the one who is evil" through trying to apply *lex talionis* to your fellow citizen, just as the Pharisees were doing.[2]

Finally, Jesus provides four examples of how the Jewish religious leaders of His day were trying to arbitrarily turn more sins into crimes than God's law allows. How do we know which is which? Breaking a statute that does not have a penal sanction attached to it qualifies as *sin*, while violating one that does qualifies as a civil *crime*. All four of Messiah's examples—a slap to the face, taking a tunic as part of a lawsuit, being forced to carry luggage for a Roman soldier up to one mile, and refusing beggars and borrowers—represent terribly selfish sins against one's neighbor that come close to being crimes without actually being crimes. For example, the entire concept of mediating interpersonal disputes via the court system is 100 percent foreign to Yahweh's law of liberty. This is why the apostle Paul prohibits believers from engaging in lawsuits against each other:

> When one of you has a grievance against one another, does he
> dare go to law before the unrighteous instead of the saints? Or do
> you not know that saints will judge the world? And if the world
> is to be judged by you, are you incompetent to try trivial cases?
> Do you not know that we are to judge angels? How much more,
> then, matters pertaining to this life! (1 Corinthians 6:1-3).

---

[2] See John Gill, *Gill's Bible Commentary*, Matthew 5:38, Kindle Location 239909.

This is also why he beseeches the Philippians to intervene in the dispute between two sisters in their congregation, to help them resolve their differences in a godly manner, and so be reconciled once more (cf. Philippians 4:2-3). Therefore, our Lord instructs us to respond to our fellow brother and civilian with mercy and kindness when he seeks to turn God's law into a weapon against us, and so "heap burning coals on his head," as the Teacher puts it (Proverbs 25:21-22). To be clear, this doesn't mean there isn't a place for contract law, concerning property for example—Proverbs is replete with teaching on this.[3] Nor does this mean there isn't a place for the victim to gently and respectfully call his brother to repentance for trying to turn a sin into a crime, and so abuse God's law. However, this does in fact mean there's no room for the victim to entertain bitterness or vengeful anger in his heart towards the civilian who's wronged him. After all, this is exactly the attitude of the scribes and Pharisees, leading them to assert themselves as civil governing authorities over their neighbors when they in fact were not, which Jesus roundly condemns.

All of this careful categorizing of God's law in the Older Testament, and how it gets explained and applied in the Newer Testament, is truly critical to the formation of a robustly consistent biblical world-and-life-view, especially as it pertains to the civil sphere. Indeed, this is not a novel view, for it's the one broadly espoused in all historic Reformed confessions—whether they be the Second Helvetic Confession, Belgic

---

[3] E.g. Prov. 6:1-5, 11:15, 17:18-20, 22:26-27.

Confession, Scottish Confession, or the French Confession—and most particularly in the three Puritan confessions: the Westminster Confession, Savoy Declaration, and the Second London Baptist Confession. This is what we find at Chapter 19 of the WCF:

1. God gave to Adam a law, as a covenant of works, by which he bound him and all his posterity to personal, entire, exact, and perpetual obedience; promised life upon the fulfilling, and threatened death upon the breach of it; and endued him with power and ability to keep it.

2. This law, after his fall, continued to be a perfect rule of righteousness; and, as such, was delivered by God upon mount Sinai in ten commandments, and written in two tables; the first four commandments containing our duty towards God, and the other six our duty to man.

3. Beside this law, commonly called moral, God was pleased to give to the people of Israel, as a Church under age, ceremonial laws, containing several typical ordinances, partly of worship, prefiguring Christ, his graces, actions, sufferings, and benefits; and partly holding forth divers instructions of moral duties. All which ceremonial laws are now abrogated under the New Testament.

4. To them also, as a body politic, he gave sundry judicial laws, which expired together with the State of that people, not obliging any other, now, further than the general equity thereof may require.

5. The moral law doth forever bind all, as well justified persons as others, to the obedience thereof; and that not only in regard of

the matter contained in it, but also in respect of the authority of God the Creator who gave it. Neither doth Christ in the gospel any way dissolve, but much strengthen, this obligation.

This view of the law led the Puritans of the seventeenth century to then insist on the separation of church and state as two separate, though related, spheres of societal authority, both being instituted by King Jesus to serve Him directly under His unlimited Messianic authority. We can find the outworking of this in Puritan works like *Lex Rex* by Samuel Rutherford.[4] Dr. Boot notes, "This principle of the *lex talionis* is central to a Puritan understanding of judicial justice and penology. It bears repeating however, that properly understood, as Jesus declares, it did not constitute an endorsement of revenge or retaliation in criminal matters in the personal sphere—quite the contrary."[5]

This discussion about the law, and its internal distinction between sins and crimes, begs the question, "Who is responsible for dealing with which aspect of breaking God's law?" Thus, the necessary separation of church and state as two distinct though related jurisdictions under Christ. To this we turn in the next chapter.

---

[4] See Samuel Rutherford, *Lex Rex: The Law and the King*, Moscow, ID: Canon Press, 2020.

[5] Joseph Boot, *The Mission of God*, pg. 315.

CHAPTER 7

CHURCH AND STATE: TWO DOMAINS UNDER KING JESUS

Two questions are now at the fore in our exploration of authority and ethics in society: First, if the nuclear family unit is the fundamental building block of society, then how does both the state and the local congregation grow out of it? And second, if God's law sharply delineates between "sins" and "sins that are also crimes," then which governmental sphere is responsible for dealing with the former aspect of violating God's law as delegated by the Lord Jesus, and which is responsible for the latter?

REFUTING WORLDLY "CHURCH & STATE SEPARATION"

Our Western so-called "enlightened" culture claims that "church and state separation" equals "God and state separation." This arises from the mainstream secular worldview, which to a large extent has successfully framed the discussion regarding scientific inquiry by pitting faith against reason. They argue that "mythical" religion must remain in a corner—locked shut behind the iron doors of privatized personal, family, and church piety—while "enlightened" reason may have free reign in all corners of the public square, whether it be business, arts, or politics. This view assumes that it's possible for people to approach any given source of information or cultural domain as a morally neutral entity, completely absent of any faith precommitments—a blank slate as it were. Smuggled into this equation, however, is its own inherent self-refutation. To say that we're morally neutral creatures who are able to come to the table with nothing but pure mechanical reason is itself a doctrine, indeed a faith assumption. What do I mean? This assertion assumes an entirely material world where we're nothing more than large bits of protoplasm, firing off random chemical reactions, and bobbing along without meaning in a purposeless universe that doesn't care about us. How this worldview gives rise to logic (which is immaterial, by the way) I have no idea! These are the secular-humanist's self-contradictory faith precommitments driving his claim of moral neutrality in the public square.

Sadly, many modern Christians have adopted this version of church and state separation and have therefore abandoned the Bible's perspective of life and the world at this critical juncture. Matthew 5:13-16 is a passage that explicitly links the progress of Messiah's kingdom rule in the world back to the mandate to transform creation into God-glorifying culture, and many modern Christians have attempted to magically turn passages like this into a kind of privatized, spiritual-only rescue mission.

This has also led to large sectors of the evangelical and Protestant world abandoning the call to consistently bring the law and gospel to bear in the public square. As Dr. Boot observes:

> This means that sincere Christians within a confessing church community may believe themselves to be essentially orthodox as far as the essential tenets of the faith are concerned, while at the same time holding to a radical progressive, liberal-democratic or even Marxist view of cultural and political life for the public space — frequently without ever recognizing a basic contradiction with their confession. In short, their ecclesiasticized confession of faith has not been mediated or contextualized to cultural and political life through a scriptural worldview in a systematic, coherent way.[1]

By way of example, this is one of the primary reasons we have not had a single law here in Canada for the past fifty years prohibiting the wholesale slaughter of innocent human beings in the womb. This is in fact *our* fault as those who confess to follow Messiah—we have disobeyed the command to "Rescue those who are being taken away to death; hold back those who are stumbling to the slaughter" (Proverbs

---

[1] Joseph Boot, *Ruler of Kings: Toward a Christian Vision of Government*, London: Wilberforce Publications, 2022, pg. 119.

24:11). We must fall on our faces with sackcloth and ashes before a holy God and with truly sorrowful and contrite hearts, cry out to Him for mercy and forgiveness, and then boldly enter the culture fray to assert the crown rights of King Jesus in defense of our preborn neighbors, even in the legislature.

PRESENTING GOD'S "CHURCH AND STATE SEPARATION"

Jesus clearly taught that, "Whoever is not with me is against me, and whoever does not gather with me scatters" (Matthew 12:30). This means that, at a heart level, there is no neutrality anywhere. All the thoughts of our minds, words of our mouths, and work of our hands is the outgrowth of the condition of our heart and the expression of that which our heart treasures the most—either in humble and loyal worship of Messiah Jesus, or in rebellious opposition to His rule. This is what the law of God teaches us, since "Everyone who makes a practice of sinning also practices lawlessness; sin is lawlessness" (1 John 3:4). Therefore, it's entirely impossible to approach any issue from the standpoint of moral and religious neutrality. This is the theological assumption behind Chapter 19 of both the WCF and 2LCF.

At the close of the previous chapter, I quoted from the WCF, Chapter Nineteen, paragraphs one through five concerning the Reformed and Puritan understanding of God's law. This is important to recognize because the following matters of Christian liberty and conscience (Ch. 20), lawfully taking oaths (Ch. 22), the civil magistrate

(Ch. 23), covenanting in marriage (Ch. 24), and the local church (Ch. 25), all theologically depend on how we understand the law, whether rightly or wrongly. The framers of the Confession recognized this dependency and so structured it in this logical order.

We can see this most clearly in the question of whether the church or state is responsible for dealing with sins as opposed to crimes. It may be easiest to understand how this works biblically through a case study. In order to reach the heart of the matter, let's use instances of rape as an example. In Deuteronomy 22:25-27, we have a case where both the congregational and civil governments are required by God's law to intervene in a terrible act of attacking the image of God in another, one that's both a sin and a crime. The question is, "Who is responsible for dealing with the sin aspect versus the crime aspect?"

We already know from Matthew 5:38-42 and Matthew 15:1-9 that the scribes and Pharisees loved to play fast and loose with the categories of church and state on the basis of the *Mishnah*, which meant that they ended up with more authority in more areas than is actually lawful. Strangely, this didn't seem to prevent them from recognizing this distinction when bringing Jesus to true civil authorities for trial and punishment. We also know from the Sermon on the Mount that Jesus came to uphold and fully obey the Older Testament ethical imperatives, instead of abolishing them (Matthew 5:17-20). We see this in His application of the civil due process of Deuteronomy 19:15-21 to the local congregation at Matthew 18:15-20. St. Paul later reaffirms this application in 1 Timothy 5:19. Evidently Jesus is upholding the former, since

He's now applying it to the latter. So, what's the difference? The difference is one of purpose and duties.

On the one hand, due process in the church is meant to deal with *sin* with the goal of Spirit-induced repentance and reconciliation, both with God and with those offended neighbors. It's meant to be restorative for everyone involved. This is an act of mercy because it seeks to deal with the sinful heart, not merely the outward act, as it pertains to those within the congregation. Accordingly, the unrepentant sinner is meant to be treated as an unbeliever through excommunication since he's acting as though he doesn't have the Spirit of God, and is thus handed over to Satan (cf. Matthew 18:17). Why? "For the destruction of the flesh, so that his spirit may be saved in the day of the Lord" (1 Corinthians 5:5).

On the other hand, the purpose of due process in the state is meant to deal with *crime* with the goal of state-induced punishment for the guilty in order to uphold the image of God in the victim and his family—it's *punitive* toward the guilty, but restorative toward the victim. It's also meant to scare others away from attempting the same thing (cf. Deuteronomy 19:20-21). It's clear that mercy toward the offender is not in view here, since God commands the plurality of civil judges (magistrates): "Your eye shall not pity" and "You shall do no injustice in the court. You shall not be partial to the poor or defer to the great, but in righteousness shall you judge your neighbor" (Leviticus 19:15) True justice is blind and treats everyone as equal before the law. This is an act of justice because it's only concerned with the outward manifestation of violating the image of God in others on a societal level. What then is

God's standard of civil justice? Yahweh's judicial standard is *lex talionis (the law of retribution)*, which was first established as part of the dominion mandate regiven in the Noahic covenant (Genesis 9:5-6), and then expressed as "It shall be life for life, eye for eye, tooth for tooth, hand for hand, foot for foot." This principle is applied in various ways including paying back double for thefts (cf. Exodus 22:4) and requiring equal weights and measures in business (cf. Deuteronomy 25:13-16). At the heart of *lex talionis* is upholding the image of God, which is why Deuteronomy 19 teaches the presumption of innocence in civil investigations and court proceedings. As mentioned previously, we see this principle applied elsewhere as well: the presumption of health until physical evidences are established by a trained medical practitioner (cf. Leviticus 13) and the presumption of innocence of a church member or leader until two to three lines of true witness and testimony are established by a plurality of ecclesiastical judges (elder-pastors) (cf. Matthew 18:15-20, 1 Timothy 5:19).

While serving in Malawi, I saw what happens when the line between these categories is blurred. Many Christians there constantly confuse the purpose and duties of the state with those of the local church. While on the one hand they think the job of the state is to make a person penitent of his crime through imprisonment—something only God the Holy Spirit has the power to do—on the other hand they believe that the job of the local church is to punish those found guilty of a sin. This is often established on the basis of smoke rather than real testimony and witness. The mindset on the part of the guilty becomes, "As long as I'm amiable and cooperative for my six-month or year-long punishment, then I can come back and continue where I left off." When such a confusion takes place, the local congregation ends up overstepping its God-given bounds and so fails to fulfill its role of authority. Likewise, when the state oversteps its bounds, and so neglects its God-given role, it also disobeys King Jesus. In such a case, the end result is that the congregation has failed to administer mercy in response to the truth, and the state has failed to administer justice in response to the truth—the victim of rape receives neither mercy nor justice, but rather further victimization.

Currently in our unjust society, the penalty for rape or sexual abuse is a lengthy prison sentence in order to force the guilty one's heart to change. This is a torturous, dehumanizing, and idolatrous approach—something to which God's Word is deeply opposed. Not only are prisons unbiblical because they don't exist in Scripture, but also because they're torturous and dehumanizing, since they lock criminals in cages like animals, when they're created in the image of God. In addition, they're unjust towards the victim, because he is made a victim a second time by the state through taxation for his offender's room and board. Furthermore, they're idolatrous because, as penitentiaries, they aim at doing what only the Holy Spirit can do, which is to create penitence in a sinner's heart. However, contra the concept of penitentiaries, biblical justice brings retribution to the convicted criminal, while upholding the image of God in him, and thereby brings restoration to the victim and his family. In a just social order under the rule of Christ, believing civil magistrates would want to act as the servant of God in society according to their mandate, which would influence unbelieving magistrates to externally do the same. This means they would be codifying God's law as the law of the land, as it applies in our context today, including *lex talionis* (cf. Romans 13:1-4). This means that in a social order like Cromwellian England, early America, and early Canada as a Dominion of the British Empire, rape would be a capital crime. The image of God in the victim has been attacked to the same level as in the case of murder (cf. Deuteronomy 22:25-27). This means that in a just society (just as with any other sin that is also a crime in God's eyes), when the ecclesiastical authorities are through with what Jesus requires of them regarding rape and sexual abuse, the civil authorities are required to obey Jesus in their part of the equation. In such a case as rape, these two forms of due process would most likely be in operation concurrently. In this way Jesus commands the local church to deal with the unrepentant sin of violating God's law, and the state to deal with the crime.

Although the Newer Testament authors focus much more on how the congregation ought to respond to sin, we can see that a just society under the rule of King Jesus, as brought about through the repentance and faith of both citizens and rulers, was certainly in their sights. For example, we can see this in the apostles claiming Jesus as Lord and Savior over and against Augustus (cf. Acts 4:12) and in their preaching of the gospel to kings, like Agrippa (cf. Acts 26). Clearly, in their minds, the mercy of the church and the justice of the state are not mutually exclusive—both are required, since Jesus as God's Messiah is not only the head of His body, the church (cf. 1 Corinthians 12:12-13), but also the "Ruler of kings on earth" (Revelation 1:5).

Dear friend, I submit to you that this ancient, confessional way of thinking about the separation of the local church and the state—as two distinct, but related bodies within society under God, both having grown out of the nuclear family—is the most consistent and biblical way of understanding this important issue. You see, Jesus as God's Messianic King has not only been given all authority over heavenly and spiritual matters, but also over earthly, physical concerns (cf. Matthew 28:18). Indeed, He's in the business of reconciling all of creation as an integrated unity, and He fully accomplished this reconciliation in His death on the cross (cf. Colossians 1:19-20). Truly, a new heart really does result in an entirely new life in Christ—not only in the church, but also in the civil sphere! As the good folks at Christ Church in Moscow, Idaho would summarize this Puritan and Kuyperian vision of reality: "All of Christ, for all of life, for all the world!"

In my next chapter, I hope to address the passage of Holy Writ that was most abused during the "Covid era" (2020-2022), that being Romans Chapter Thirteen. I hope to provide a consistent reading of the text, one that respects its context, not only within St. Paul's letter to the Roman believers, but also within the whole flow of Scripture. I'm intentionally bringing this up in the eighth chapter instead of the first because I believe this passage assumes and builds upon everything I've addressed so far. Let's turn to the thirteenth chapter of Romans.

CHAPTER 8

GOD'S DESIGN FOR THE STATE: ROMANS 13 UNBOUND

Over in Moscow, Idaho, there resides a most despised scoundrel among evangelicals, a Christian thinker who doesn't mind rocking the boat of modern traditions and sensibilities in a jovial and respectable sort of way. The jovial scoundrel I'm referring to is of course Douglas Wilson, Christ Church's senior minister.[1] Now, once a year Doug lays aside his usual qualifications and politeness when writing posts on his blog, *Blog and Mablog*. During *No Quarter November*, he

---

[1] See *Christ Church*, Our Staff & Leadership, https://www.christkirk.com/our-church/leadership-staff.

hoists his proverbial Jolly Roger, ignores parley, and joyfully turns completely piratical in unashamedly calling "a spade a spade" and launching direct firebrand assaults at the heads of our cultural idols and unbiblical traditions. For the month of November, and this month alone, he sets aside all his softer tools of communication and fully unsheathes his Elijahic serrated combat sword.[2] While we should never foster an attitude of being needlessly incendiary or vindictive toward others, there is a biblical place wherein love for neighbor demands joyously "hoisting the Jolly Roger," vigorously "rocking the boat," resolutely "burning the ships," and aggressively "poking the bear." One may rightly ask, "which time would that be?" One such time would be when our modern traditions and/or sensibilities have been planted squarely in the way of Christ's people fully obeying Him. I mean to suggest that we've now arrived at such a time in the culture war here in the West. This is my one-chapter "No Quarter November," as it were.

OUR MODERN CONTEXT

We live in a day where the popular interpretation of Romans 13 is representative of a widespread mindset that says, "The world should be divided into 'sacred' (religious) and 'secular' (irreligious)—the 'sacred' is private while the 'secular' is public." Usually this means that God's law is restricted to Newer Testament ethics only, applying to the "sacred," while

---

[2] See *Mostly Peaceful No Quarter November 2020*, https://www.youtube.com/watch?v=nBEnaNOFMR8, *No Quarter November 2021 | Doug Wilson*, https://www.youtube.com/watch?v=zQgfbhTRl3I, and *No Quarter November 2022*, https://www.youtube.com/watch?v=o5j0AclzORA.

man's reason applies everywhere "secular." While this may sound reasonable to many, it actually fails to conform to reality and is thus objectively false. First of all, as the Creator incarnate, Jesus taught, "Whoever is not with me is against me, and whoever does not gather with me scatters" (Matthew 12:30). The apostles affirm this, saying, "For the mind that is set on the flesh"—sinful nature—"is hostile to God, for it does not submit to God's law; indeed it cannot. Those who are in the flesh cannot please God" (Romans 8:7-8). It is clear: there is no neutrality! Our hearts are either facing King Jesus in glad submission or turned away from Him and rebelliously warring against Him through some kind of false worship. There is no halfway in-between. It doesn't matter whether someone's station in life be carpenter, banker, pastor, or politician—this is true regardless.

Furthermore, to claim that God now tolerates two ethical standards—one that He's given in His infallible, holy Word unto His people and one that comes from the fallible, unholy reasoning of sinful man—is to make God out to be both changing and unjust in His character. Proverbs 20:10 says, "Unequal weights and unequal measures are both alike an abomination to [Yahweh]." Truly, Yahweh abhors double standards. Why? He is true justice in and of Himself. Are we to say then that Jesus changed the Father's mind on this point, even though He said, "Whoever relaxes one of the least of these [Older Testament] commandments and teaches others to do the same will be called least in the kingdom of heaven" (Matthew 5:19)? By no means! Indeed, we must learn to humble ourselves and think Yahweh's thoughts after Him, submitting even our most deeply held traditions to His infallible, holy Word, no matter how uncomfortable it may feel to do so. If we're not careful, Jesus' rebuke to the Pharisees in Matthew 15 will begin rightly applying to us as it did them.[3]

GETTING TO THE ROOT OF THE MATTER

During the Covid era (2020-2022), we heard much in our broadly evangelical and Protestant circles about the need for submitting to the civil governing authorities as unto God, and this on the basis of Romans 13:1-7. While I would give a hearty "Amen!" to civilians needing to submit to their governing authorities as unto Christ—in the same way that children must do so with their parents and congregants with their elder-pastors—going down this road only serves to obfuscate the real issue. Unless one is a committed anarchist, which most Christians are not, the question is not *whether* the state has been given authority from God to rule its jurisdiction but in *which* way. The question is not *whether* citizens must obey their civil authorities, but in *which* way. In order to prop up their obfuscation, many church leaders made reference to Romans 13:1-7, assuming the validity of the popular understanding of the text without actually taking the time to properly work through the text with believers, both within its immediate and cross-canonical contexts. This was devas-

---

[3] In Matthew 15:1-9, Jesus rebuked the scribes and Pharisees for hypocritically forcing the Scriptures to submit to their oral tradition (the *Mishnah*) rather than submitting their tradition to the Scriptures. In so doing, they proved that, though they would say otherwise, they loved the *Mishnah* as ultimate over and against God's very Word, and so made mincemeat out of it.

tating for many of Christ's sheep over the course of the Covid crisis, those very sheep for whom He bled and died.

What do I mean? I submit to you that the modern, popular understanding of Romans 13:1-7 is based on a faulty reading thereof. First, those advocating it try to read this portion in isolation, as though it can be properly understood all by itself without any consideration of what comes before or after. This is a violation of how the letter was written, indeed how all Newer Testament epistles were originally written. When St. Paul wrote his epistle to the Romans, it was written as one continuous text. Truly, it wasn't until much later that spaces between words, punctuation, and paragraph divisions were introduced for the ease of reading, and even later when chapter and verse divisions were introduced by John Calvin's printer, Robert Estienne (in Latin, *Stephanus*).[4] Therefore, attempting in any way to read this portion in isolation from the rest of St. Paul's letter constitutes an abuse of the text.

Second, by taking this approach, these advocates read Romans 13 in a simplistic, cursory fashion that ends up forcing it to contradict other parts of Scripture. What do I mean? They would say that since God has given the civil magistrate the authority to come up with laws that seem best to him and so rule in a manner that seems reasonable to the majority, it is incumbent upon Christians to unquestioningly obey him, even funding him through taxes, across the board.[5] To paraphrase

---

[4] See Britannica, *Robert I Estienne: French Scholar and Printer*, https://www.britannica.com/biography/Robert-I-Estienne.

[5] This is the view for which Kirk Wellum argues in his paper entitled *Dr. Martyn Lloyd-Jones on Church and State as Articulated in his Exposition of Romans 13:1-7*, https://

Todd Friel, "Even if they were to mandate wearing a pinwheel on the sides of our heads, we must obey!"[6] Ironically, this view forces the Christian to agree with the statist when he claims that the state is the fundamental building block of society and should therefore possess an absolutist, authoritarian kind of rule. This really is idolatry of the state. However, as we saw back in Chapter Five, this is contrary to reality as defined by the Creator and Sustainer of reality Himself. The totality of God's Word—even down to treating the crime of treason as being against the family government rather than the civil—militates hard against big governments and their need to micromanage society according to their own unbelieving, sinful, and rebellious reasoning processes. Again, there is no neutrality anywhere in God's good world.

Furthermore, to add insult to injury, modern advocates of this simplistic, authoritarian reading of Romans 13 insist that the only exception to this rule would be a direct gun-to-the-temple demand of the civil magistrate upon the Christian civilian to deny Jesus as the divine Messiah, his personal Lord and Savior. Unfortunately, as noble as this may sound to those who think church history started with Billy

---

uploads-ssl.webflow.com/6271486b6928786a8e6fcef4/641a002f2a1ab864ef8f20f6_ GPF%202023-03-06_Martyn%20Lloyd-Jones%20-%20Kirk%20Wellum.pdf.   His basis for this seems to be drawn from David VanDrunen's *[Radical] Two Kingdom Theology*, which seeks to drive a wedge between the "sacred/redemptive" kingdom, where God's law applies, and the "common/creational" kingdom, where natural common sense reasoning applies. The former is a morally charged realm, while the latter realm is morally neutral with no opportunity of being transformed into the former — they are forever parallel tracks.
[6] Doctrinal Watchdog, *I'm going to cut Todd Friel down to size says James White / Rebuked Over Romans 13 Pinwheel Comment*, https://www.youtube.com/watch? v=F9pJ6TFhGWw.

Graham, the reality is that this only serves to dishonor the memory of many thousands of persecuted and martyred believers down through the centuries. How? By ignoring the historical circumstances under which they suffered for the sake of Christ, which in no way fit the impossibly narrow parameters of modern evangelicals.

For example, are we to say that our first- and second-century brothers were not actually persecuted? After all, the Roman civil government arrested them as "atheists" and enemies of the state—those who refused to honor Caesar as the ultimate authority in the Empire, even above all gods. Few if any of them had a single Roman soldier come and stick a blade to his throat, demanding him to deny the deity of Christ Jesus. The authorities didn't care who you worshipped, just as long as the Emperor was Number One. Shall we then say that the author of Hebrews was wrong to advise his readers to "Remember those who are in prison, as though in prison with them, and those who are mistreated, since you also are in the body" (Hebrews 13:3)? Whether we like it or not, ideas do in fact have far-reaching consequences, ones we cannot ignore if we are to be honest and even-handed followers of the Lord Jesus. We do, after all, claim to belong to the One Who is "the way, and the *truth*, and the life" (John 14:6, emphasis added).

ROMANS 13 UNBOUND

How shall we then rightly understand this significant passage of Holy Writ within its God-given context? What was the message that St. Paul was trying to communicate to his Roman audience 2,000 years ago? This is the question that demands a robust, consistent answer. At the outset, it's important to notice that we've entered into the "So what?" section of St. Paul's letter—the first eleven chapters were a systematic unpacking of the Gospel, while the subsequent five are an application of that good news to everyday life. Concerning the passage at hand, the apostle logically begins this particular portion of application back at 12:9, rather than at 13:1.

The apostle exhorts, "Let love be genuine. Abhor what is evil; hold fast to what is good" (12:9). This begs the question, "By what standard?" What is the plumbline or level by which we may know what the apostle Paul means by "love," "evil," or "good"? We don't have to look very far, not even beyond this very letter; the apostle has already defined God's standard of righteousness and justice back in Chapters One and Two. After demonstrating how all people everywhere naturally hold down the truth of their Creator and Judge in unrighteousness, St. Paul provides a list of vices and concludes with these words: "Though they know God's righteous decree that those who practice such things deserve to die, they not only do them but give approval to those who practice them" (Romans 1:32). How exactly do all men naturally know right from wrong, as well as the eternal consequence for practicing the wrong? The apostle answers this question in Chapter Two. He explains that, while Jews had the advantage of possessing the codified version of God's law as His covenant people, Gentiles remain without excuse because they also have the very same law written in their hearts as fellow image bearers of Yahweh, which daily informs their conscience. It's by this one standard of righteousness that all men everywhere at all times will be judged by their Creator on the Last Day (cf. Romans 2:12-16). What's the content of that perfect law? Again, St. Paul answers this question—it is God's own holy character as summarized in the Ten Commandments, the first table defining "love for God" and the second table defining "love for neighbor" (cf. Romans 2:21-24). In this way, since the author to the Romans has already defined his terms, from 12:9 onward "love," "good," and "evil" are defined by the contents of Yahweh's moral and unchanging law.

The apostle Paul then applies this principle to the situation of ordinary civilians interacting with one another. We find this in Romans 12:14-21. These verses include ethical sayings like, "Bless those who persecute you," "Live in harmony with one another," "Repay no one evil for evil, but give thought to do what is honorable in the sight of all," "Beloved, never avenge yourselves, but leave it to the wrath of God, for it is written, 'Vengeance is mine, I will repay, says the Lord,'" and "Do not be overcome by evil, but overcome evil with good." All of this is quite Sermon-on-the-Mount-esque.

Now, considering that in the following verses the apostle transitions from the duties of civilians toward one another to those of the civil magistrate toward civilians, it seems clear that he specifically has Matthew 5:38-42 in mind. Why? There we find our Master utilizing Older Testament ethical categories, the most important of which being the distinction between "sins" and "crimes." This is a part of his application to all of life concerning his saying in Romans 12:9, "Let love be genuine.

Abhor what is *evil; hold fast to what is good.*" Therefore, this application in verses 14-21 is specifically directed to civilian believers in how to deal with other civilians. This does not seek to address the relationship between civilians and governing authorities, as many pastors and teachers have tried to force it to do. How do we know? Because that's what the apostle Paul addresses next.

St. Paul continues to apply his thesis when he says, "Let love be genuine. Abhor what is evil; hold fast to what is good," in Romans 13:1-7. Here, instead of instructing civilians on how they are meant to relate to other civilians as under the kingdom rule of Messiah Jesus, he now instructs civil magistrates on how they are meant to relate to civilians as unto God, since they are meant to be His deacon (servant) in society.[7] Given the already established structure to this passage, it's clear that the apostle does not have a specific historic situation in mind (e.g. Nero's reign), but is prescribing the way this relationship *ought* to function across the ages. How do we know? St. Paul's usage of "love," "good," and "evil" throughout this passage is defined by God's immutable, holy law, which is rooted in His immutable, holy character.

Getting into the meat of how this relationship is supposed to work, it is clear that the apostle Paul is primarily addressing believing civilians in how they are meant to respond to their civil governing authorities. For example, verses 1-2 decimate any notion that Christians may become

---

[7] See John Gill, *Gill's Bible Commentary*, Romans 13:1, Kindle location 306119. Gill recognizes a difference between the subject matter in Chapter Twelve and here in Chapter Thirteen when he says, "the former chapter contains his Christian Ethics, and this his Christian Politics."

anarchists—submission to the state is submission to God Himself, since He's the one Who put them in their place of authority as His deacon in society. In verse 3 he exhorts the civilian, "Would you have no fear of the one who is in authority? Then do what is good, and you will receive his approval, for he is God's servant for your good." Finally, in verses 6-7, the apostle instructs them to cooperate in funding the state to carry out their responsibilities, as God's instituted servant in society.

At the same time, embedded in this application, St. Paul secondarily addresses Christian civil magistrates in how they are meant to rule over civilians, as unto God Himself. How do we know that he's treating these governing authorities as believers? Because he tells them they are meant to be serving King Jesus through their duties of promoting the good and punishing the evil as God's appointed earthly avenger (cf. verse 4). Who defines "the good" and "the evil"—the one appointed or the One appointing, the servant or the Master? Obviously, the Master defines the duties of the servant, as well as the ethical standard by which they are meant to be carried out. Who truly desires to serve King Jesus and obey His law-Word in all that it teaches—believers or unbelievers? St. Paul has already answered this question for us in Romans 2:28-29 and 8:6-8. In the former text he says, "For no one is a Jew who is merely one outwardly, nor is circumcision outward and physical. But a Jew is one inwardly, and circumcision is a matter of the heart, by the Spirit, not by the letter. His praise is not from man but from God." Again, in the latter he explains, "For to set the mind on the flesh"—sinful nature—"is death, but to set the mind on the Spirit is life and peace. For the mind that is set on the flesh is hostile to God, for it does not submit to God's law, indeed it cannot. Those who are in the flesh cannot please God." It is therefore clear that, as per the law, the apostle Paul is now setting forth the standard for how governing authorities ought to rule in society. It is a standard that can only be obeyed to any degree from the heart by those truly regenerated, and so united to Christ, by His Spirit.

Now, what exactly are the duties of God's appointed civil governing authorities? Well, they certainly do not include concocting their own inherently unjust rules and regulations and then imposing them on everyone else in society. God forbid! Rather, their duty is to humbly and gladly submit themselves in all they do to the totality of God's already revealed law-Word and then do as He commands.[8] What exactly is His purpose for the civil magistrate? To bear the sword of retribution in their allotted jurisdiction. Verse four says, "But if you do wrong, be afraid, for he *does not bear the sword in vain*. For he is the servant of God, an *avenger* who carries out God's wrath on the wrongdoer" (emphasis mine). By what standard? By the standard of *lex talionis*, first established in the post-fall republication of the original creational covenant (cf. Genesis 9:5-6), and then applied as God's standard of justice throughout the Mosaic law. Since Deuteronomy 19:15-21 is King Jesus' design for civil due process, which necessarily involves applying the principle of retributive justice to various situations by the state, the civil magistrate is restricted to upholding only those laws with penal sanctions attached to

---

[8] See John Gill, *Gill's Bible Commentary*, Romans 13:3, Kindle location 306192.

them, not those without. It is the state's role to deal with *crimes* committed in society, while *sins* ought to be dealt with by the local church. Therefore, the civil magistrates' entire role is coercive in nature, since they must apply the general equity of God's law to modern situations, both in terms of legislation, and in terms of judicial sentencing and punishment. In this way, by using God's law justly, the civil magistrate restrains real evil in society and teaches society the moral values they ought to have (cf. 1 Timothy 1:8-11).

Only in acting as Jesus' deacon in society may the civil government tax the people residing within their allotted jurisdiction, through the least coercive means possible, for the accomplishment of the aforementioned specific duties and no more. This and only this is what Messiah Jesus obligates civilians to cheerfully and respectfully fund as it pertains to the civil government. Why? Because this alone is what rightfully belongs to the civil magistrate—he has no other God-given duty. This is the specific type of civil government St. Paul commands civilians to respect and fund—one that is acting as God's deacon (servant): "For because of this you also pay taxes, for the authorities are *ministers of God*, attending to this very thing"—encouraging "the good" and punishing "the evil," as per God's law. "Pay to all what is *owed* to them: taxes to whom taxes are owed, revenue to whom revenue is owed, respect to whom respect is owed, honor to whom honor is owed" (Romans 13:6-7, emphasis added). This is why Jesus said, "Render to Caesar the things that are *Caesar's*, and to God the things that are *God's*" (Luke 20:25, emphasis added). We all must live in God's world in the way He has prescribed, including those serving in the state, and we all must give an account at the final judgment for how we have sought to or failed to do so.

St. Paul concludes this section of his epistle to the Roman congregation by circling back around to his original point in Romans 12:9. He instructs, "Owe no one anything, except to love each other, for the one who loves another has fulfilled the law. For the commandments, 'You shall not commit adultery, You shall not murder, You shall not steal, You shall not covet,' and any other commandment, are summed up in this word: 'You shall love your neighbor as yourself.' Love does no wrong to a neighbor; therefore love is the fulfilling of the law" (Romans 13:8-10). If there was any confusion as to what he meant by "Let love be genuine. Abhor what is evil; hold fast to what is good," he now makes it explicitly clear. This is Yahweh's one and only standard of ethics for all men everywhere until the end of the world, whether they be civilian or civil magistrate.[9]

FURTHER CONSIDERATIONS

God's Word teaches that we're all accountable to each other, since we're all living in God's world together under the righteous rule of King Jesus. The call of the gospel is equally for each and every one of us: to turn from our law-breaking as it manifests itself in the particular stations of life in which we have been providentially placed, and to turn and cling to Mes-

---

[9] See John Gill, *Gill's Bible Commentary*, Romans 13:8, Kindle location 306272.

siah Jesus with the empty hand of faith for eternal peace with God, forgiveness and mercy for our sins, and true life found only in Him. And then, with new hearts that now love God and love His law, we gladly and loyally follow King Jesus in His narrow way by obeying His good law as it applies to our various stations of life. In this way, civil magistrates must obey Messiah Jesus and must be instructed in how to properly and consistently do so from the totality of God's law-Word, just like the rest of us (cf. Matthew 28:18-20). I therefore suggest to you that it's the duty of faithful Christians to teach members of the governing authorities their God-given role and then call them to repentance and faith in Christ on particular points of violating that role. Furthermore, for the Christian to cooperate with a state that is in open defiance of the one, true, and Triune God is a heinous sin that requires repentance in a hurry. Why? To cooperate with a civil government that demands it be treated as the ultimate, unlimited authority in society is in fact wanton idolatry of the state. The Scriptures are clear, "we must obey God rather than men" (Acts 5:29). Indeed, this is what John Knox had in mind when he famously said, "Resistance to tyranny is obedience to God."[10]

So, how exactly can we measure when our governing authorities are beginning to leave behind God's infallible, just law in favor of man's fallible, unjust law? What are some indicators that our civil magistrates are shedding their role as God's civil servants to robe themselves in tyranny,

---

[10] See Megan Tien, *God and Politics: John Knox and the Scottish Reformation*, The Uc Santa Barbara Undergraduate Journal of History, Vol. 1, No. 2, Fall 2021, https://undergradjournal.history.ucsb.edu/fall-2021/tien.

which is state-enforced lawlessness? God's Word again does not leave us wanting: they call what King Jesus calls righteous, unrighteous, and what He calls unjust, just; they try to usurp King Jesus' rightful place as the ultimate authority and provider over all; they begin conscripting civilians for military duty rather than letting them voluntarily enlist; they try to use their power to own and control more and more property in the land; women are convinced to serve in governmental roles of leadership and/or combat, rather than as the nurturers and caretakers in their family context as God has designed them to be; taxation is 10 percent or higher; and people cry out to God for help, but He does not listen because we as a nation wanted a government that hates His holy rule (cf. Deuteronomy 22:5, 1 Samuel 8:10-18). Since all of these things, and much more, are currently true in Canada—as is true in other Western nations—we can know that as a nation we're in the process of being judged by our Creator and Judge. We desperately need nationwide, Spirit-induced repentance, spiritual renewal, and reformation from the bottom to the top of our social order. May this true revival begin with the household of God!

In moving forward, I hope to outline some of the major rules for thinking Christianly about jurisprudence. While continuing to operate on the biblical categories already established thus far, I will focus on the ways in which the transition from the old covenant age to that of the new covenant affects our understanding of how the law applies to us today. While I cannot hope to provide you with every single example, which is beyond the scope of this book, I can give you highlights as a preamble.

CHAPTER 9

RULES FOR CULTURAL AND POLITICAL REFORMERS: PART I

I can hear it now: "I thought we as Christians were supposed to be all about the Gospel. Isn't concerning ourselves with cultural transformation straying too far from our mission as outlined in the Great Commission, especially as such transformation manifests itself in the civil sphere?" I would respond, "Not as long as our Messiah's incarnation, life, death, resurrection, current session, and eventual return on the Last Day remains the reference point in thinking through our transformational efforts." Why? Jesus Himself recognized that as God's Anointed King, He had arrived not only to bring about the eternal salvation of all those the

Father had given Him but also to usher in His kingdom rule over all nations, to rescue the whole of creation from the curse of the fall. Do you remember history's very first promise of the Gospel? Genesis 3:15 promised that while the devil would bite the heel of the woman's future Son, that Son would in fact be victorious in crushing the head of the devil, thus destroying all evil in the world. In summarizing the good news of Jesus' death and resurrection unto glory, the apostle Paul gives us a snapshot into what this actually looks like. He says, "Then comes the end, when he delivers the kingdom to God the Father *after* destroying every rule and every authority and power. For he must reign *until* he has put all his enemies under his feet. The *last* enemy to be destroyed is death" (1 Corinthians 15:24-26, emphasis added). Elsewhere he explains, "For in him all the fullness of God was pleased to dwell, and through him to reconcile to himself *all* things, whether on earth or in heaven, making peace by the blood of his cross" (Colossians 1:19-20, emphasis added). This good news certainly *does* include the redemption of particular sinners, but it *also* includes the redemption of everything else in creation that humans are involved with! Thus, Jesus' Messianic mission is far greater than merely the personal lives of you or me.

This is the Gospel of the kingdom that Jesus preached when "he went throughout all Galilee, teaching in their synagogues and proclaiming the gospel of the kingdom and healing every disease and every affliction among the people" (Matthew 4:23, 9:35). This is the kingdom rule into which one can only recognize and enter by the Spirit's transformative work in granting him the new birth (cf. John 3:1-8). And this is the kingdom rule, together with the righteousness and justice of that kingdom, we have been commanded to trustingly seek first in everything we do as Messiah's followers (cf. Matthew 6:33). In light of this, being involved with Gospel-driven cultural transformation is not optional for the faithful Christian. As R.J. Rushdoony once put it, "A piety which concerns itself only with man's soul and leaves the world to the devil is a profane piety."[1]

With that said, what are some guiding principles for the believer in applying biblical law to modern circumstances? For example, what are we meant to do with blasphemy laws? What about wearing more than one type of fabric in a garment or eating shellfish? How do we deal with the sacrificial system? I think the easiest way to address these kinds of issues would be to deal with each table of the law, one at a time. Throughout, I will seek to consistently apply the principle of "later revelation is given to interpret, explain, and apply former revelation," as per the Reformational hermeneutic, *analogia fide (the analogy of faith)*.

DEFINING OUR TERMS

Deuteronomy 5:7 records Yahweh's command, "You shall have no other gods before me." This is applied judicially in Deuteronomy 17:2-7, "If there is found among you, within any of your towns that [Yahweh] your God is giving you, a man or woman who does what is evil in the sight of [Yahweh] your God, in transgression of His covenant, and has gone and

---

[1] Rousas J. Rushdoony, *An Informed Faith: The Position Papers of R.J. Rushdoony*, Vol. 1, pg. 327, Vallecito, CA: Ross House Books, 2017.

served other gods and worshipped them…you shall inquire diligently, and if it is true…you shall stone that man or woman to death with stones. On the evidence of two witnesses or three witnesses the one who is to die shall be put to death; a person shall not be put to death on the evidence of one witness…So you shall purge the evil from your midst." How are we meant to responsibly deal with this, since the old covenant administration has been permanently done away with and we're now under the new covenant? We cannot simply brush this aside—this is God's good and holy law-Word after all (cf. 2 Timothy 3:16-17).

The question is not *whether* but *which*—it's not *whether* blasphemy laws still exist, but in *which* way. We currently have blasphemy laws in Canada—when it's blasphemy against the individual, it's called "hate speech" and when it's against the state, it's called "domestic terrorism." In fact, formerly a Christian nation, Canada had true blasphemy laws on the books. The most famous relevant trial in Canadian history concerned a certain Eugene Sterry of Norwich, England who had moved to Toronto in 1926 and was arrested on charges of blasphemous libel against the one, true, and Triune God of Holy Scripture on 10 January 1927.[2]

You see, there's always a deity of the system to which glory and sacrifice is demanded. The question is, "If the state is Jesus' deacon (servant) in its jurisdiction and He alone is the true ultimate authority in society, does that mean we must have state-codified and state-enforced laws against blaspheming the one, true, and living God?" This is a good

---

[2] An article on this story can be found at, https://digitalcommons.law.ggu.edu/cgi/viewcontent.cgi?article=1141&context=annlsurvey.

question, one that demands an exegetical answer, rather than a tradition-ally- or emotionally-based response. Just because Canada, and Cromwellian England prior to her, did indeed attempt to make God's law the law of the land (no matter how imperfectly she did so) does not necessarily mean that we must do likewise. Indeed, what it *does* mean is that Christians in fairly recent history did in fact think that creating a distinctly Christian civilization was a good and God-honoring idea.

In order to address this question, it seems best to begin with two underlying questions. First of all, what is the biblical purpose of law in the civil sphere and has that purpose in any way changed due to the con-summation of the covenant of grace in the new covenant? Second, what is the significance of worship in the context of social and cultural devel-opment? Understanding the Scriptural answers to these questions will provide a framework for approaching the issue at hand.

To begin with, what is the purpose of law in the civil sphere? Here, Calvin is quite helpful. In thinking through this question, he demon-strates how the Bible teaches three uses of God's law: (1) as a means of building a well-ordered society under the rule of Christ, (2) as a means of convicting the unbeliever of sin, leading him to Christ, and (3) as a means of teaching the believer the way of godliness and piety.[3] As it per-tains to the first use of the law, which is our present concern, in what way is it a means of building a well-ordered society under the rule of

---

[3] See A. Cairns, *Dictionary of Theological Terms*, The Law of God, The Purpose and Uses of the Law, Belfast: Ambassador Emerald International, 2002. Sourced at https://reformed.org/definitions/law_of_god.html.

Christ? It seems the biblical answer to this question is twofold—as a restrainer of evil, as well as a teacher of righteousness.

The first way that it functions is as a restrainer of evil in society. We have already seen this in Chapter Eight. Romans 13:3-4 teaches,

> For rulers are not a terror to good conduct, but to bad. Would you have no fear of the one who is in authority? Then do what is good, and you will receive his approval, for he is God's servant for your good. But if you do wrong, be afraid, for he does not bear the sword in vain. For he is the servant of God, an avenger who carries out God's wrath on the wrongdoer.

By what standard is the "good" and the "wrong" determined? By the immutably righteous and just statutes of the one, true, and living God. Evil as thusly defined can only be restrained by the same law which defined it. No other standard will do. Why? Only heartfelt obedience to God's law is truly loving to Yahweh and our fellow man, since it's the codification of His very character. All other standards of justice are created by fallible men and will inevitably be as prone to corruption and abuse of others as those who devised them. Jesus' law is inherently just and a blessing to the nations, while man's law, whichever version it may be, is inherently unjust and a catalyst to oppression and tyranny. Rushdoony is helpful here: "In a fallen world, with men in revolt against God, God's law is the only effective and valid check against evil, the only true way of justice, and the necessary condition of life."[4] There is no middle ground. There is no neutrality.

The second way the law functions in society is as a teacher of righteousness, that is, a cultural instructor in the kind of morality a society ought to value, the kind of morality that is truly pleasing to the Lord Jesus. In a way, the first use of the law is a broader application of both the second and third uses, but on a civilizational scale. Those in the Reformed and Puritan tradition have long argued for this use of the law from 1 Timothy 1:8-11 where the Apostle Paul teaches:

> Now we know that the law is good, if one uses it lawfully, understanding this, that the law is not laid down for the just but for the lawless and disobedient, for the ungodly and sinners, for the unholy and profane, for those who strike their fathers and mothers, for murderers, the sexually immoral, men who practice homosexuality, enslavers, liars, perjurers, and whatever else is contrary to sound doctrine, in accordance with the gospel of the glory of the blessed God with which I have been entrusted.

To begin with, St. Paul says "the law is good, if one uses it lawfully." Many modern Christians think that God's law is somehow a throwaway now that we are under the grace of the Gospel—all that's required of us is "love for God" and "love for neighbor," which we are somehow free to define for ourselves. However, the apostle forcefully rejects this antinomian way of thinking. He then goes on to list the second table of the

---

[4] Rousas J. Rushdoony, *The Institutes of Biblical Law*, Vol. 3, pg. ix, Vallecito, CA: Ross House Books, 1999.

law, in order no less, which he says the violation thereof is "contrary to sound doctrine." He even includes specific applications of the moral law, like "striking one's father and mother," "men practicing homosexuality [sodomy]," and "enslaving [man-thieving] others," which are all found in the Mosaic case law system. Clearly, the Newer Testament authors viewed the Older Testament ethical imperatives as fully binding on all men everywhere at all times. This is the grounds for legislating God's law in society as a means of instructing the nations in what we ought to value as truly righteous and just, and so live by. Lastly, St. Paul makes a beeline from the law to the Gospel. After having clearly stated that "the law is not laid down for the just but for the lawless and disobedient," he says this is "in accordance with the gospel of the glory of the blessed God with which I have been entrusted." This is the good news he has systematically and painstakingly laid out in the first eleven chapters of his epistle to the Romans. Only by the atoning work of God the Son on the cross in the place of all those God the Father had given Him in eternity past—as applied to the sinner by God the Spirit through regeneration, creating in him a living, repentant faith unto justification—is it possible for anyone to love Yahweh, love His law, become a son of the kingdom and enter therein, and so come to follow the Son in His narrow way. Attempting to obey the law never has, nor ever will rescue anyone from his own rebellious heart and the just wrath of the Almighty—only God's sovereign grace in the Gospel can do that.

Likewise, just as only true believers are sons of Messiah's kingdom rule, only true believers are able to advance His kingdom rule to the ends of the earth, whether it be through building godly businesses, creating godly and beautiful art, blessing others with well-made tools, or working to legislate God's law as the law of the land in ways that honor and magnify Him.[5] Wherever the devil has raised up gates of hell in society and culture, it's up to the church of the living God to be the battering ram of King Jesus against those ideological strongholds, asserting His crown rights over them so they fall (cf. Matthew 16:18; 2 Corinthians 10:3-6). In all these things, it is God's Word which remains the only fully authoritative, sufficient, and ultimate standard at each and every step along the way. To paraphrase Dr. Joseph Boot, "The Scriptures are God's kingdom charter for all of life," not merely for the personal and ecclesiastical spheres.[6] Thus, it is specifically within this context and in this way that we see the purpose of God's law in setting the ethical tone of a society and so teaching the nations the values of Messiah's kingdom they ought to have from the heart.

Since we have tackled the question of the purpose of God's law in the civil sphere as implemented during the new covenant age, it's now time to turn our attention to the question of worship within the context of social and cultural development. It has rightly been said, "You become what you worship." Once again, it's not a matter of *whether*

---

[5] A great example of how this can be done well can be seen in the Phoenix, Arizona-based company, *Armored Republic*, https://www.ar500armor.com. Another good example would be the art produced by *Every Good Work*, https://everygoodwork.art; This in no way means that unbelievers living amongst believers cannot benefit from or externally imitate their kingdom culture-making. They can and they do. But, unbelievers are unable to advance Christ's kingdom with godly motivation, for such requires the new birth.

[6] See Ezra Institute for Contemporary Christianity, *Are Christianity & the West Doomed? | Joe Boot & Jeff Durbin*, https://www.youtube.com/watch?v=kk6HmuSW38g, 27:53.

image bearers will worship, but to *which* deity we will render glory and sacrifice—will it be to the one, true, and living God of the Bible, the Creator of heaven and earth, or will it be to some false god, an idol reflecting elements of the created order? "The human heart is a constant idol factory," as John Calvin so aptly put it.[7]

Consider with me the 115th psalm. The psalmist opens with the refrain, "Not to us, O Yahweh, not to us, but to Your name give glory, for the sake of Your steadfast love and faithfulness!" He then proceeds to spend much of the psalm contrasting Yahweh, the one true God, with all the false gods of people's imaginations. The punchline is found in verse 8, "Those who make them become like them; so do all who trust in them." Timothy Tennent explains:

> This is a great reminder to us. If you worship a dead block of wood or stone, you will become like what you worship, dead and lifeless. If you worship the living God, you will become like Him, with all His vibrancy, relationships, and character.[8]

Would the Lord our God have our society dedicated to giving glory and sacrifice to idols and false gods in hot rebellion against Him— whether it be Shiva or Vishnu, Buddha or the Self, Allah or other Unitarian conceptions of monotheism, the self-actualizing individual or the state, sex or money? Or would He have our civilization dedicated to

---

[7] The Master's Seminary, John Street, *Enslaved: A Theology of Addiction*, https://blog.tms.edu/enslaved-a-theology-of-addiction.
[8] Seedbed, Timothy Tennent, *We Become Like What We Worship: Psalm 115*, https://seedbed.com/we-become-like-what-we-worship-psalm-115.

right worship in glad allegiance to Him alone, He Who is the one, true, and Triune God of Holy Writ, our Creator and our Judge? We cannot have it both ways—it can only be one or the other. As Dr. Greg Bahnsen repeatedly reminds us, "Neutrality is a myth."[9]

This is the problem with the concept of *multiculturalism*, isn't it? While there's certainly nothing wrong with allowing those of other ethnic backgrounds to join another nation's established citizenry—certainly, all our families once came from elsewhere—the cultural Marxists want to hijack this allowance to force equality of cultural values, as though each and every one of them is as morally valid as the next. This kind of radical egalitarianism latent in all forms of Marxism has led to a transformation of the God-given right of *freedom of religion* into a ghastly, beastly creature. The founding fathers of both Canada and the United States intended to prevent the federal government from establishing a state church as has been done in places like Germany, Denmark, and England. This was to prevent the state from interfering in the worship of individual Protestant congregations. In a similar yet corrupt fashion, cultural Marxists have successfully bastardized *freedom of religion* in the minds of Westerners to now mean "freedom of idolatry."[10] This kind of chaos is what ensues when we abandon the Lord Jesus

---

[9] Markus GH, *The Myth of Neutrality — Dr. Greg L. Bahnsen*, https://www.youtube.com/watch?v=L9Jc5b56NtU.

[10] An example of this can be seen in Pierre Trudeau's *Canadian Charter of Rights & Freedoms*, Section 10: General, https://www.justice.gc.ca/eng/csj-sjc/rfc-dlc/ccrf-ccdl/pdf/charter-poster.pdf.

as the one, true ultimate authority over all of life, including the public square. In reality it's either Christ or chaos—there are no other options.

THE FIRST TABLE OF THE LAW

In light of all of the above, what must we do with the first table of the law as it pertains to the civil sphere? What must we do with public expressions of worship to false gods, like the building of mosques and yoga studios? What should we do with public attacks on the one, true, and Triune God, as Mr. Sterry did in his atheistic agenda?[11] If we are to be consistent and faithful, we must look into God's law-Word and come to understand what *He* requires as it pertains to the first use of the law, that is, as it pertains to building an orderly society under the rule of God.

This is the word of Yahweh:

> You shall have no other gods before me. You shall not make for yourself a carved image, or any likeness of anything that is in heaven above, or the earth beneath, or that is in the water under the earth. You shall not bow down to them or serve them; for I [Yahweh] your God am a jealous God…You shall not take the name of [Yahweh] your God in vain, for [Yahweh] will not hold him guiltless who takes his name in vain (Deuteronomy 5:7-10).

These are the first three Commandments. Moses applies these civilly in Deuteronomy Chapter Twelve, where he commands Israel not to tolerate the presence of pagan religions in the land through practicing state-sanctioned iconoclasm, that is, they must tear down every public

---

[11] Refer to Eugene Sterry's story above on pg. 44.

expression of false worship in the land (cf. Deuteronomy 12:1-4). This was the response of every righteous king in Israel when they wholeheartedly returned to God's law (e.g. Hezekiah in 2 Kings 18), while the response of every evil king was to go after false gods (cf. 1 and 2 Kings). We know obedience to this command wasn't meant for national Israel only, since Moses had earlier explained:

> See, I have taught you statutes and rules, as [Yahweh] my God commanded me, that you should do them in the land that you are entering to take possession of it. Keep them and do them, for that will be your wisdom and your understanding in the sight of the peoples, who, when they hear all these statutes, will say, 'Surely this great nation is a wise and understanding people.' For what great nation is there that has a god so near to it as [Yahweh] our God is to us, whenever we call upon Him? And what great nation is there, that has statutes and rules so righteous as all this law that I set before you today? (Deuteronomy 4:5-8).

Now, this doesn't mean that all the nations of the earth were to become carbon copies of Israel, as though they also were nations in covenant with Yahweh in the exact same way Israel was. Rather, they were meant to leave their national covenants with false gods and turn to covenant with Yahweh instead, openly acknowledging Yahweh as the only true God and ultimate authority over them. Within this context, they were meant to imitate the ethical standards which were given to bless Israel and the nations around her, as applicable in their specific contexts.

Furthermore, as noted above, Deuteronomy 17:2-7 requires:

> If there is found among you, within any of your towns that [Yahweh] your God is giving you, a man or woman who does what is evil in the sight of [Yahweh] your God, in transgression of his covenant, and has gone and served other gods and worshipped them...you shall inquire diligently, and if it is true...you shall stone that man or woman to death with stones. On the evidence of two witnesses or three witnesses the one who is to die shall be put to death; a person shall not be put to death on the evidence of one witness...So you shall purge the evil from your midst.

"Going and serving other gods and worshipping them" involved ascending the high places and going before Asherah poles to publicly worship Canaanite gods. What's clear is that any move in the direction of judicial penalties against idolatry required following civil due process—the charge must be established on the basis of two or three true witnesses before a plurality of judges, as found in Deuteronomy 19:15-21.

This means that in a just and God-honoring society (as per the law's general equity), all public places of worship to false gods—whether Hindu or Sikh temples, Islamic mosques or New Age yoga studios—must be torn down, stone off of stone. This would also include Unitarian places of worship like Oneness Pentecostal churches and Jehovah's Witness Kingdom Halls, since they likewise are worshipping false gods. Furthermore, anyone found guilty, through the due process of law, of attempting to rebuild a torn down place of false worship or of attempting to recongregate the public worship to a false god would be deserving of the death penalty. Why? "So you shall purge the evil from your midst." Notice that the issue here is the *public*, not the private, worship of idols. God's law does not advocate for "witch hunts" whereby the police must go through each and every home in search of idolaters. Why? That which society as a whole tolerates or doesn't tolerate is a reflection of the moral standard it actually holds and wishes to set as an ethical tone for all. Furthermore, the law doesn't have the power to change anyone's heart. While it's meant to *restrain* public expressions of idolatry, it *cannot* compel anyone to worship the one, true, and living God—only the regenerating work of the Holy Spirit has the power to so change a person's heart. Thus, in a just society where biblical law is the law of the land, evangelism of the heathen and unbelieving is still very much a necessity.

In addition, Leviticus 24:15-16 instructs, "And speak to the people of Israel, saying, Whoever curses his God shall bear his sin. Whoever blasphemes the name of [Yahweh] shall surely be put to death. All the congregation shall stone him. The sojourner as well as the native, when he blasphemes the Name, shall be put to death." This is a civil application of the Third Commandment. Again, the issue here is the *public* blaspheming—mocking and attacking—of the Triune God, His name and His character. This means that, upon being found guilty through the due process of law, Mr. Eugene Sterry ought to have been executed by the state for the crime of blasphemous libel, as per God's law.

So then, in what manner should such lawful executions take place? In the swiftest and most humane way possible, while also being performed publicly (cf. Deuteronomy 19:20; 21:22-23; Ecclesiastes 8:11). What's important about it being swift and humane? Although judicially guilty of a crime, the condemned person is still a bearer of God's image, and thus has inherent dignity, value, and worth that must be upheld (cf. Genesis 9:5-6). Indeed, God's law is firmly opposed to torture of any kind. Likewise, why must it be performed *publicly*? To put the fear of God in the hearts of others, so they will be deterred from trying the same thing. Practically applied in today's context and in keeping with the general equity of the law, this requires a due process that's thorough in establishing an accused person's guilt or innocence, with as few delays as possible. The defendant would be allowed to submit one, and only one, appeal to the judges the week after the verdict, for example, so that the sentence may be enacted as soon as possible to avoid perverting justice (cf. Leviticus 19:15). This also means the condemned person must be executed in the quickest, least painful way possible. For example, a hanging by the neck—the science of a proper hangman's knot, combined with the proper length of rope in relation to the weight and height of the person being hanged, will kill him on impact. Finally, this means that it must take place in a context where the public may freely observe, whether within the courthouse or without.

The final law I will address in this chapter is that of Sabbath Day observance. Yahweh commands, "Observe the Sabbath day, to keep it holy, as [Yahweh] your God commanded you. Six days you shall labor and do all your work, but the seventh day is a Sabbath to [Yahweh] your God...." (Deuteronomy 5:12-15). Exodus 20 makes it clear this command did not originate in the old covenant, but rather in God's act of creation, "For in six days [Yahweh] made heaven and earth, the sea, and all that is in them, and rested on the seventh day. Therefore [Yahweh] blessed the Sabbath day and made it holy" (Exodus 20:11). Here in Deuteronomy 5, Moses says that by keeping it, "You shall remember that you were a slave in the land of Egypt, and [Yahweh] your God brought you out from there with a mighty hand and an out-stretched arm. Therefore [Yahweh] your God commanded you to keep the Sabbath day" (Deuteronomy 5:15). The reason why all men every-where must now keep the Sabbath Day holy is for the same reasons, as typologically fulfilled in Messiah's death and resurrection. Not only is the Sabbath Day rooted and grounded in Yahweh's creational acts at the beginning of history, but also in His new creational acts initiated in raising His Son from the dead. And not only is it meant to be a remembrance of Israel's redemption by the preincarnate Son of God out of Egypt, it is a remembrance of true Israel's redemption out of slavery to sin and death by Jesus the incarnate One. We must keep it from sundown on Saturday to sundown on Sunday because "there remains a Sabbath rest for the people of God, for [he who] has entered God's rest has also rested from his works [in his resurrected glory] as God did from his [upon completing his work of creation]" (Hebrews 4:9-10). The WCF puts it this way:

> As it is the law of nature, that, in general, a due proportion of time be set apart for the worship of God; so, in his Word, by a positive, moral, and perpetual commandment binding all men

> In all ages, he hath particularly appointed one day in seven, for a
> Sabbath, to be kept holy unto him: which, from the beginning
> of the world to the resurrection of Christ, was the last day of the
> week; and, from the resurrection of Christ, was changed into the
> first day of the week, which, in Scripture, is called the Lord's
> Day, and is to be continued to the end of the world, as the Chris-
> tian Sabbath.[12]

Furthermore, as it pertains to its civil application, Exodus 35:1-3 specifically makes Sabbath-breaking a civil crime and not merely a sin. This is the word of Yahweh: "Moses assembled all the congregation of the people of Israel and said to them, 'These are the things that [Yahweh] has commanded you to do. Six days work shall be done, but on the seventh day you shall have a Sabbath of solemn rest, holy to [Yahweh]. Whoever does any work on it shall be put to death. You shall kindle no fire in all your dwelling places on the Sabbath day.'" In the modern context, this means all businesses and shops of any kind must remain closed from sundown Saturday until sundown Sunday. Only those most necessary occupations—such as law enforcement, firefighting, ambulance services, and basic hospital operations—may continue on through the Sabbath out of mercy for those in the most dire and urgent of needs.

Why does God take the breaking of His Day so seriously in sanctioning it with the death penalty? First, it's an act of ingratitude to the God Who gives us every breath and the very created order in which we live and move and have our being. Second, it's an attack on the goodness

---

12 WCF, 21.7.

of the God in Whose image we are made, the God Whom we are meant to imitate in turning His good creation into culture that glorifies and enjoys Him forever. And finally, it's an act of ingratitude for making us freemen in Christ through the Gospel, by preferring slavery instead—slaves are made to work every day, while freemen aren't. This was the logic behind the Lord's Day Act here in Canada, even during the 1980s. The God of creation is the God of the covenant, and He will not give His glory to another (cf. Isaiah 48:11).

In the next chapter, I hope to address how the second table of the law applies to reforming culture and politics today. While the second and third uses of the law are vitally important, so also is the first, and this is the particular usage I wish to focus upon, just as I have done in this chapter.

CHAPTER 10

RULES FOR CULTURAL AND POLITICAL REFORMERS: PART II

In Part I, we considered how the transition from the old covenant to the new covenant impacts the way in which the first table of the law is applied to us today. We discovered that Yahweh continues to take very seriously the attack on His character, including how it pertains to the first use of the law. As we're about to see, the same is true when it comes to the second table of God's most holy, unchanging law. Indeed, the cooperation between the two spheres of authority, state and church, still remains in addressing sins that are also crimes. Why? While the church's role is to mercifully respond to unrepentant *sins* in the congregation through the church discipline process, the state's role is to justly respond to *crimes* in its jurisdiction via civil due process. Both church and state must obey King Jesus within their delegated spheres of authority.

THE SECOND TABLE OF THE LAW

Cornelius Van Til once said, "The Bible is authoritative on everything of which it speaks. Moreover, it speaks of everything."[1] This is what 2 Timothy 3:16-17 is getting at, which we must remember was first given to Timothy in reference to the *Tanakh*—the Older Testament Scriptures. This means that the typical evangelical response, "We're not under law, but rather grace"—as if the Older Testament has virtually nothing to say to the way we must live today—must be rejected. If we're to think Christianly, we must be careful to follow biblically established categories, in the same way the Bible interprets itself, with later revelation interpreting, explaining, and applying what was given earlier. The following is a case study for the sake of demonstrating how this works biblically.

Deuteronomy 5:16 reveals the Fifth Commandment, "Honor your father and your mother, as [Yahweh] your God commanded you...." We see this applied in the Mosaic case law system in multiple ways. For example, Deuteronomy 21:18-21 commands, "If a man has a stubborn and rebellious son who will not obey the voice of his father or the voice of his mother, and, though they discipline him, will not listen to them..." his parents must take their son to the civil authorities to be

---

[1] Cornelius Van Til, *The Defense of the Faith*, Philadelphia: Presbyterian & Reformed, 1955, pg. 29.

tried and convicted for rebellion. The examples given in the text are glut-tony (riotous eating) and drunkenness, which function not as the statutory crime itself, but as judicial descriptors of a settled, incorrigible pattern of rebellion. The son has become morally worthless—lawless and destructive—which is what the Hebrew term zālal denotes. These traits reveal a life of dissipation, contempt for authority, and the squandering of the household's goods. Ironically, they are also forms of idolatry, since they turn food and drink into objects of devotion, seeking satisfaction from them rather than from God (cf. Colossians 3:5-6).

It is clear that the parents have faithfully discharged their covenantal duty to discipline and instruct their son, raising him in the way he must go. Yet now, though he has reached maturity—the age of marriage—and has been given repeated opportunities to repent, he con-tinues in outright refusal to listen or receive godly correction. In the familial sphere, such hardened rebellion would warrant disinheritance; in the ecclesial sphere, it would call for excommunication. In the civil sphere, however, where persistent rebellion against lawful authority con-stitutes public crime, the due penalty is capital punishment—that is, state-sanctioned execution (v. 21).

Why must the penalty be execution? Because a son or daughter's ongoing, incorrigible rebellion against the God-given authority of parents is treason against the family government itself. If left unchecked, such treason does not merely harm a household; it undermines the very foundation of social order, resulting in the destruction of society rather than its flourishing. Why is the Fifth Commandment applied in this way?

As was discussed in Chapter Five, the family government is the foundational building block of society. For this reason, Moses explains in verse 21, "So you shall purge the evil from your midst, and all Israel shall hear, and fear." Since only two chapters earlier, these words were uttered in the context of judicial due process (cf. Deuteronomy 19:19-20), we can see that Moses is assuming the same here as well.

Now, lest anyone accuse me of wanting to transplant Mosaic law into the present wholesale (i.e. the judicial execution of rebellious sons must take the form of stoning), let me quote from the WCF, "To them also, as a body politic, he gave sundry judicial laws, which expired together with the State of that people, not obliging any other, now, further than the general equity thereof may require."[2]

In other words, while the outward form was binding to the nation of Israel with which Yahweh covenanted at Mt. Sinai, the inward principle remains binding for us today, since it's merely an extension of His moral law (as it pertains to image bearers living together in society). In the same way that Jesus did not "come to abolish the Law or the Prophets"—the *Tanakh*—"...but to fulfill them" (Matthew 5:17), He Himself upholds the distinction in the law between sins and crimes (cf. Matthew 5:38-42), and He Himself instituted the civil magistrate to be His servant in society to exact His vengeance on the wrongdoer through upholding His standards of justice (cf. Romans 13:1-7). We must therefore say that the substance of the God-given penal sanction, together with the substance of the God-given statute itself, is unchanging until

---

[2] WCF, 19.4.

the end of the world and is equally binding today as it was to Israel. As Dr. Joe Boot points out, law is both precept and sanction together—we cannot separate the two.[3] This means that the Lord Almighty requires the civil magistrate today to uphold the totality of Deuteronomy 21:18-21 in its general equity, not picking and choosing which aspects he wishes to apply legislatively and judicially and which ones he doesn't. He must uphold the image of God in the accused by employing cross-examination techniques that do not in any way include torture and, if convicted, the guilty must be swiftly executed in the most humane way possible (cf. Deuteronomy 21:22-23; Ecclesiastes 8:11). He is King Jesus' servant, and a servant must obey his Master. Doing otherwise will necessarily result in dishonoring his Lord and in abusing his neighbors, and he will be required to give an account for this on the Last Day.

WHAT ABOUT SHELLFISH?

The issue of the holiness code is always a sticking point for sceptics of the faith, but it shouldn't be for us as Christians. The Scriptures are clear both as to the purpose of this type of statute, and how the principle those statutes were teaching is applied under the new covenant.

Deuteronomy 14:1-21 explains which types of animals Jews under the old covenant were allowed to eat and which ones were prohibited. Among land creatures, Israel was restricted to eating those that both

---

[3] Joe Boot and Ryan Eras, *Podcast for Cultural Reformation*, Slavery, Law, Crime and Punishment, https://www.ezrainstitute.com/resource-library/podcast/slavery-law-crime-and-punishment, 13:35.

chewed the cud and had cloven hooves—all else was off limits. Among sea creatures, they were restricted to those with both fins and scales—all else was to be excluded. Among flying creatures, they were prohibited from eating those that lived by eating the flesh of creatures that had naturally died, which they were also prohibited from doing. Permitted creatures were "clean" and those prohibited were "unclean." But why? Was the issue at hand health concerns, as some have supposed? The text explicitly tells us…twice! Verse 2 explains the reason, "For you are a people holy to [Yahweh] your God, and [Yahweh] has chosen you to be a people for his treasured possession, out of all the peoples who are on the face of the earth." Again in verse 21 Moses says, "You shall not eat anything that has died naturally. You may give it to the sojourner who is within your towns, that he may eat it, or you may sell it to a foreigner. *For you are a people holy to [Yahweh] your God*" (emphasis added). The purpose was to draw a clear line of delineation between Israel and the pagan nations around them, since Yahweh had chosen them to be His own treasured possession in His free and sovereign grace. And, since cutting oneself for the dead (verse 1) is included in the list, we know this reasoning extends to all clean and unclean regulations in the law, not merely ones pertaining to food.

What about today? The old covenant was made first and foremost with the nation of Israel, which historically came to a jolting end with the desolation of the temple and the holy city in AD 70. Yet, followers of Jesus today are not under the old covenant, since they belong to the new covenant administration of the covenant of grace—that one historic covenant community down through the ages—which has expanded to include both Jews and Gentiles who are covenantally united with their Head, the Lord Christ Jesus. So, how does this work? In the first century, the Jerusalem Council convened to address this very issue. We can read about this in Acts Chapter Fifteen. On the basis that *both* Jews and Gentiles "will be saved through the grace of our Lord Jesus," having *both* been given the same Holy Spirit, "having cleansed their hearts by faith" (Acts 15:7-11), they determined that only the aspects of the holiness code applying to both groups should remain. Thus, we're required to "abstain from the things polluted by idols, and from sexual immorality, and from what has been strangled, and from blood" (vs. 20). This is the summary of what Lev. 17:10-19:8 teaches. Ultimately, the reason these things are universally binding is that they are rooted in the covenant Yahweh made with all His image bearers at creation and then republished in light of the fall in the Noahic covenant (cf. Genesis 9). So, despite what many Christians have been taught, we do in fact have a holiness code today, but one rooted in creation, rather than in being uniquely tied to Israel's life in the Promised Land.

Furthermore, the apostle Paul argues in like manner in 1 Corinthians 6:12-20. As those who belong to Messiah Jesus by faith, "your body is [now] a temple of the Holy Spirit within you, whom you have from God," and he applies this creationally based holiness code to the issue of sexual ethics. Why does it matter whether or not "[our] body is a temple of the Holy Spirit"? It matters because the image of God is in the process of being restored in us, since we're now covenantally united to the true Image of God, the Lord Jesus (cf. Romans 8:29, Colossians 1:15). This is absolutely incredible! Not only this, but St. Paul's line of reasoning seems to indicate that the distinction between "clean" and "unclean" in the old covenant was given as a kind of "training wheels" for the people of God to learn the concept of separation from ungodliness. But now as image bearers in Christ, we're treated as adults who are expected to wisely discern how to apply this principle in keeping with the dominion mandate with the enabling help of the Holy Spirit to Whom we now belong, body and spirit. In this way, what's revealed earlier in Scripture is explained and applied by that which is revealed later.

WHAT ABOUT SACRIFICES AND PRIESTS?

Lastly, we come to the aspect of the Mosaic law most consistently recognized as typological by all branches of Bible-believing Christians, namely, the ceremonial laws. Hebrews 7-10 is the most important section of Holy Writ concerning this subject, since it deals with it directly. The author to the Hebrews, by the moving of the Holy Spirit, explains that Jesus is the far better High Priest that the previous Levitical priesthood was pointing toward because He belongs to a better priesthood, one that allows Him to "hold his priesthood permanently, because he continues forever" (Hebrews 7:24). Not only this but, as that great High Priest, Jesus has established a new and better covenant with His people by way of His death on the cross, one "enacted on better promises" (8:6). Indeed, as the true High Priest, He offered Himself as the once-for-all-time perfect sacrificial Lamb in the place of all His people, all those the Father had given Him in eternity past (cf. 9:15). In this way, Jesus secured for them personally their eternal redemption, something the blood of bulls and goats could not do—sacrifices were previously given as shadows pointing forward to their realities in the person and work of Messiah (cf. 10:1-4). Finally, as our High Priest, Jesus took the perfect blood of His own sacrifice and entered into the Most Holy Place in heaven to present it to His Father for acceptance, whereupon He permanently sat down on the Mercy Seat to effectually pray into reality everything which He fully accomplished in His death (cf. 9:11-14, 10:11-18). Within the context of Hebrews as an apologetic sermon, the author to the Hebrews argues here that since we have a better High Priest, a better covenant, a better sacrifice, and a better intercession, we must not return to the former types and shadows which pointed to them, lest we deny their perfection and sufficiency.

What this means is that the ceremonial laws do in fact continue to be binding, but only as they're fulfilled in and through Jesus as our High Priest. This is expressed in the WCF thusly:

> Beside this law, commonly called moral, God was pleased to give to the people of Israel, as a Church under age, ceremonial laws, containing several typical ordinances, partly of worship, prefiguring Christ, his graces, actions, sufferings, and benefits; and partly

holding forth divers instructions of moral duties. All which ceremonial laws are now abrogated under the New Testament.[4]

In this way, the Confession recognizes the way in which later revelation interprets former revelation, and which pattern we must also rigorously follow if we are to read God's Word the same way He wrote it.

As mentioned before, Van Til taught, "The Bible is authoritative on everything of which it speaks. Moreover, it speaks of everything."[5] This most certainly includes issues of authority and ethics. We must always try, with the Spirit's help, to approach God's Word on its own terms, submitting our preconceived ideas and deeply held traditions to it, rather than the other way round. Failing to carefully do this results in situational ethics and argues against the way the Scriptures do. This is indeed a very dangerous place to find oneself. Why? To argue against the way Scripture does is to argue against God Almighty Himself. Let us all, each and every one of us, "humble yourselves before the Lord, and he will exalt you" (James 4:10).

---

[4] WCF, 19.3.
[5] Cornelius Van Til, *The Defense of the Faith*, pg. 29.

CHAPTER 11

RULES FOR CULTURAL AND POLITICAL REFORMERS: PART III

The subject of Christian penology is about as foreign to most modern evangelicals as being hunted is to sea birds. However, this has not always been so. In fact, jurisprudence has been a part of Reformational thinking since the time of John Calvin. In sixteenth-century Europe, Calvin's mentor Martin Bucer wrote:

> But since no one can describe an approach more equitable and wholesome to the commonwealth than that which God describes in his law, it is certainly the duty of all kings and princes who

recognize that God has put them over his people that they follow most studiously his own method of punishing evildoers.[1]

Furthermore, the so-called "last of the Puritans," Charles Haddon Spurgeon, wrote in nineteenth-century England:

> I long for the day when the precepts of the Christian religion shall be the rule among all classes of men and all transactions. I often hear it said, 'do not bring religion into politics.' This is precisely where it ought to be brought and set there in the face of all men as on a candlestick. I would have the cabinet and members of Parliament do the work of the nation as before the Lord...[2]

The notion that modern judicial penology must be derived solely from God's law-Word *did not* begin with Bahnsen and Rushdoony in the 1980s, as some have supposed. Rather, it's rooted in Reformational thought, particularly that of the seventeenth-century English Puritans. Boot explains the heartbeat of this outlook, "Thus theonomic Puritanism is the belief that *all of Scripture in its totality is God's covenant law-word* and as such, properly interpreted, remains in force in every detail till heaven and earth pass away. As Vern Poythress notes, 'At the heart of theonomy is the conviction that God's word is the only standard for evaluating all human action,' whether in the social, personal or judicial sphere. Such a view, theonomists hold, deserves the support of all Christians."[3] Indeed, this ethical perspective deserves thoughtful consideration,

---

[1] Martin Bucer, cited in Joseph Boot, *The Mission of God*, pg. 305.
[2] C.H. Spurgeon, cited in Joseph Boot, *The Mission of God*, pg. 308.
[3] Joseph Boot, *The Mission of God*, pg. 311.

for it's rooted both in the careful exegesis of Scripture and the historic precedence of those who diligently studied and taught the Scriptures, even being tested in the fires of some incredibly trying times. With this in mind, we come to a rather complicated aspect of Christian jurisprudence, that being determining the fitting punishment for various degrees of civil crime.

SOME PRELIMINARIES

At the outset, it's worth emphasizing four important points when considering this subject. First, we must remember we are dealing with the *first* use of the law, *not* the second or third. All orthodox Christians confess that sinners must repent of their sins and seek their forgiveness in Christ Jesus, whether they be tried and convicted criminals or not. However, this does not in any way negate the fact that civil magistrates must punish guilty convicts without the slightest partiality. It's the question of justice in the first use of the law which is at hand in this chapter.

Second, we must recall the type of justice which God commands in His Word. God's standard of justice is in no way arbitrary or preemptive, for it proceeds from His very character as Yahweh. Rather, it is retributive and fitting to the crime committed. The principle at work here is called *lex talionis (the law of retribution)* and was first introduced in the post-fall regiving of the creational covenant found at Genesis 9:5-6.

Third, the Mosaic civil law was given as a case law system, meaning that it's meant to give base examples as to how the Ten Commandments should be applied but is then left to the discretion of the judges involved to determine how best to apply the law in each particular case. Legal precedence from previous similar cases would also be a resource for the plurality of judges to consult. Within the Western legal tradition going back to King John and the Magna Carta in 1215 AD,[4] the Mosaic case law system has been the basis for English Common Law, which was transplanted into both Canada and America upon their respective foundings. This is also why we have degrees of conviction, seeing as the circumstances of any given crime vary in degree of severity.

Finally, we must remember that God's law presupposes His final judgment of all mankind on the Last Day (cf. Revelation 20:11-12). Unlike the modern mindset toward justice, God's law seeks to protect the innocent by demanding two to three lines of independent and truthful testimony in order to establish a conviction. If solid evidence is lacking, the accused person must go free, even if that means he might have escaped justice in this life. Without keeping the final judgment in mind, it would be quite easy to pervert justice as history bears witness.

With these four points in mind, how then do we go about determining degrees of severity in conviction, and therefore degrees of punishment that are indeed fitting and not simply arbitrary? And more

---

[4] Due to the tyranny of King John in thirteenth-century England, the Magna Carta was drafted by the Archbishop of Canterbury as a means of putting Scriptural restraints on the monarch. Though King John reluctantly signed it and later broke it, the Magna Carta established a legal precedent in the West in opposition to the "divine right of kings." See Trinity Bible Chapel, *Church at War Breakout: Constitutional Heritage Part 1 with André Schutten*, https://www.youtube.com/watch?v=xv3j9mI5k9o and Trinity Bible Chapel, *Church at War Breakout: Constitutional Heritage Part 2 with André Schutten*, https://www.youtube.com/watch?v=ErTnpWmC7M4.

to the point, how are we meant to do so as faithful Christians, standing solely on the divinely given Scriptures as our immovable standard?

DEGREES AND SANCTIONS

The legal discussion surrounding degrees of guilt in any given case can be extremely nuanced. It involves thinking carefully about the level of intent, malice, and the specific type of crime at hand. For example, as it pertains to theft, did the theft involve violence or not? If there was no violence incurred in the process of the robbery, the one found guilty must repay double to the victim. If he used or damaged what he stole, he must repay fourfold (cf. Exodus 22:1-4). If he doesn't have the means at the time of conviction, he must become an indentured servant of his victim to work for him until his debt is paid off or until the seventh year when his debt must be forgiven (Exodus 21:1-2; 22:3). However, if violence was incurred during the course of the robbery, either physical assault or murder would be added to the conviction. In the former, the guilty must be publicly flogged up to forty lashes "in proportion to his offense" (Deuteronomy 25:1-3).

When it comes to biblical law, the real question comes to sentences requiring the death penalty. What is the difference between first- and second-degree kidnapping? Under what circumstance is the death penalty required? What's the biblical penalty if not death? While critically contemplating such things has become something of a taboo for many twenty-first century believers, determining the justness of not only a conviction but also its due civil penalty in light of God's law-Word is vitally important, since it reflects either positively or negatively on the very character of God Himself. For this reason, we now consider these things.

Now, using rape as a case example, a conviction of first-degree rape would mean the one guilty had malice of forethought, meaning he planned out the specifics of the rape ahead of time with the malicious intent of violating another human being, and was indeed successful in his endeavour. However, a second-degree rape conviction would mean the one convicted acted maliciously in the moment without any fore-thought.[5] While public execution must certainly be applied to a first-degree conviction (Deuteronomy 22:25-27), a public flogging of forty lashes, and not a lash more, would be a just answer to rape of the second degree. According to Deuteronomy 25:3, there's a reason for no more than forty lashes: "lest, if one should go on to beat him with more stripes than these, your brother be degraded in your sight." As has been seen elsewhere, upholding the image of God even in the guilty is extremely important in biblical law. In this vein, using something like the Roman short whip would be forbidden, since it would cause torture and disfig-urement—Roman soldiers used "a short whip with several single or braided leather thongs of variable lengths, in which small iron balls or sharp pieces of sheep bones were tied at intervals."[6] The use of something

---

[5] See FindLaw, *The Different Degrees of Guilt*, https://www.findlaw.com/criminal/criminal-rights/the-different-degrees-of-guilt.html.
[6] Truth of God, *Scourging and Crucifixion in Roman Tradition*, https://www.cbcg.org/scourging-crucifixion.html.

like a simple short whip, minus any damage-causing objects, or a thin, flexible rod would be biblically permissible.

Again, this distinction in the application of the law would apply to other crimes requiring the death penalty as their maximum sanction. Such crimes include adultery, failing to close one's business on the Christian Sabbath, and blasphemous libel. For second-degree offenses as proven through two-to-three lines of witness and testimony in a court of law, the just penalty for the state to administer, as prescribed in God's holy Word, would be public corporal punishment of up to forty lashes in proportion with the severity of the circumstances of the crime committed. The only crime that's always biblically required to be answered with the death penalty by the state is murder (Genesis 9:5-6).

While this may seem harsh to many modern Christians, we must remember two factors. First, biblical justice is concerned with returning to a person what's proportionally *due* him. Thus, God's standard of justice is *retributive* in nature, rather than being preemptive, therapeutic, or arbitrary as we often experience in our modern context. This is precisely what prison sentences are—arbitrary and therapeutic. Second, there's a categorical difference between something being *harsh* and it being *unjust*. Again, Dr. Boot is helpful in his comments at this point:

> There is a difference between penalties seeming comparatively harsh (to modern sensibilities) and being *unjust*. Here the question again comes back to the *source and definition* of law and justice—what defines these for man? In the cultural milieu of ethical and judicial confusion today, foundation questions must

be asked afresh. What is the relation between crime and punishment? Which sins are crimes? How should various crimes be punished? Without the *specific* guidance of God's law we have no adequate answers to these foundational questions.[7]

Truly, we will either be ruled by Almighty God's perfectly just and holy standards or by some derivation of man's inherently unjust and unholy standards.

Now, how must we judicially respond to manslaughter, as opposed to murder? What is its due penalty, as we look into Holy Writ? The modern understanding of manslaughter is the unintentional taking of another's life due to carelessness.[8] Such a definition would include everything from vehicle collisions due to excessively fast driving to a child falling in an open well that should have been covered. However, God's Word places a much higher value on human life and the individual's personal responsibility for the wellbeing of his neighbor than that. Indeed, God's law requires individuals and families to think ahead of time about their neighbor's physical wellbeing and take measures for their protection when engaging in potentially risky activities. Fatalities resulting from negligence of this responsibility are considered murder as opposed to manslaughter. We can see this clearly at Deuteronomy 22:8— "that you may not bring the guilt of blood upon your house." In the eyes of God, such a derelict person ought to be charged with first-degree murder.

---

[7] Joseph Boot, *The Mission of God*, pg. 313.
[8] See FindLaw, *The Different Degrees of Guilt*, https://www.findlaw.com/criminal/criminal-rights/the-different-degrees-of-guilt.html.

However, what *is* considered manslaughter is the unintentional *and* unexpected taking of another's life. The example given in Deuteronomy 19 is "when someone goes into the forest with his neighbor to cut wood, and his hand swings the axe to cut down a tree, and the head slips from the handle and strikes his neighbor so that he dies" (verse 5). Obviously, the man in question had used the axe many times before without a problem and had carried his axe into the forest without the head falling off. The assumption is that this man is skilled in chopping wood with an axe. In this way, not only was the death of his friend unintentional, but it was also entirely unexpected. From the way the rest of the passage treats the manslayer, it's clear that before the law he's innocent of any crime and must be protected as such by the civil magistrate (verses 5-10). This is how much God's law values the image of God in us and how much it values the presumption of innocence.

If we want to see God's blessing return to the West, we must return to a thoroughly biblical vision of authority and ethics as it applies to each and every arena of life—not only as it applies to calling sinners to repentance and faith in Christ, and not only as it applies to the believer's personal walk with the Lord, but also as it applies to the civil realm and the governance of societies and nations. God's law-Word is unambiguous—as a general principle, we reap what we sow (cf. Proverbs 22:8-9). If we want to see the Lord Jesus exalted, His kingdom-rule advanced, and His blessings abound in society, we must repent of neglecting the goodness of His law and return to faithfully obeying Him in the details and do so from the heart. This is my prayer for Canada, as well as every other nation that finds itself under the judgment of Almighty God.

CHAPTER 12

ANSWERING COMMON OBJECTIONS

As the finale to this work, I would like to take some time to respond to common misconceptions, misrepresentations, and hesitations I have encountered since coming to a historic Reformed and Puritan outlook on life. I realize that many of the things of which I have explained from the text of Scripture may be quite new to many. This chapter is meant to be a help to you, to bring clarification to a view which was widely accepted as recently as two hundred years ago.

THE "LAW VERSUS GRACE" OBJECTION

Some modern Christians would reject what I have sought to demonstrate from a consistent reading of the text of Scripture with, "But doesn't John 1:17 say we are no longer under law, but under grace? Why then are you discussing the law, since it's irrelevant to us today?" They would attempt to argue the same point by appealing to a text like Galatians 5:18, "But if you are led by the Spirit, you are not under the law."

This objection in fact represents an ancient heresy known as *antinomianism*, meaning "against the law." It posits that, since we are saved by God's grace alone, we no longer need to obey the law, especially those commands found in the Older Testament. However, a significant misreading of Scripture is involved in order to arrive at this conclusion. First, John 1:17 reads, "For the law was given through Moses; grace and truth came through Jesus Christ." The entire context of John's prologue concerns Jesus the Word coming in the flesh, Who is very God of very God. The point leading into verse 17 is that "the Word became flesh and [tabernacled] among us, and we have seen his glory, glory as of the only Son from the Father, full of grace and truth." John wants his audience to understand that through His incarnation, Jesus has completely fulfilled the role the old covenant tabernacle and temple played in housing the glorious presence of Yahweh—we now see that glory in the face of Jesus the Messiah! Thus, verse 17 is emphasizing the type-antitype relationship between the tabernacle and temple, and Jesus. This has positively nothing to do with a supposed abolition of the Older Testament ethical commands.

Second, the main issue in St. Paul's epistle to the Galatians is the attempt to gain God's acceptance by way of combining the primary principle of the old covenant administration (law) with that of the covenant of grace (faith). The main text (forming an interpretive grid for the rest of the book) is Galatians 4:21-31, which explicitly teaches that Abraham had two offspring, one historic and one eschatological, but only those with Abraham's faith in the promised Messiah are truly his descendants. This concept is expressed multiple times throughout the letter, including in 3:7, "Know then that it is those of faith who are the sons of Abraham" and 3:29, "And if you are [Messiah's], then you are Abraham's offspring, heirs according to promise." This is the whole reason why circumcision, the sacramental sign of the old covenant made with historic Israel, is at the forefront of the debate between the apostles and the Judaisers. When St. Paul says, "But if you are led by the Spirit, you are not under the law" (5:18), he's contrasting the attempt to keep the law as an unregenerate member of the covenant of grace under the old covenant with the effort to do so as a Spirit-indwelt regenerate member of that same historic covenant community, but now under the new covenant. The flesh has no power to obey God's commandments, but the Spirit does! Indeed, this militates hard against any notion that God's Older Testament ethical imperatives have been annulled with the coming of the Messiah and the inauguration of the new covenant.

THE "ICKY" OBJECTION

Some believers would argue against what I have defended from Scripture on the basis that it grates hard against their modern sensibilities on an emotional level. It is usually expressed something like, "I have no problem with the first half of Leviticus 20:13—that God calls homosexuality an abomination—but I can't deal with the state giving practicing homosexuals the death penalty. That is unloving!" For those who want to keep the righteous precept but reject the just penal sanction to such a case law, I would humbly and respectfully ask, "By what standard?" Yahweh treats sodomy as a *crime* and not merely as a *sin*, yet some think His penalty is in some way "icky." With which penalty then should we replace the death penalty? In such a case, there's only two options: either the state doesn't legislate against sodomy, even though God requires this, or it legislates a penalty that's based on what seems right in its sinful common-sense way of reasoning. In both cases, we end up with injustice over and against Yahweh's perfectly just standards.

Furthermore, it's worth considering that since Christians began retreating from the public square around the turn of the twentieth century, and thus began handing 1,500 years' worth of Christian civilization over to the heathen to do with as they pleased, God's law has been progressively repealed from the Criminal Code of Canada. What happens when Bible-believing Christians cease to defend the legislation of God's law in society? We now not only have the legislated celebration of sodomite "marriages," but also the mutilation of boys and girls through trans activism, the sexual grooming of children via Drag Queen story hours in public libraries, and the soon acceptance of paedophilia and pederasty under the guise of "minor attraction."

So again I ask, Shall we reject the second half of Leviticus 20:13, but keep the first half, because our modern sensibilities lead us to pit mercy against justice, even though the Apostle Paul (in keeping with the Gospel) doesn't do this in his usage of this exact passage in 1 Corinthians 6:9-11? Are we to think that our creaturely "common sense" form of justice is somehow more civilized, and therefore more just, than Almighty God's? Indeed, if this is our attitude, we must repent of such wanton pride and then take steps to guard against it through the power of the Holy Spirit.

THE "QUAINT" OBJECTION

Finally, still others would argue that since we possess technology, scientific discoveries, and the like (which did not exist 4,000 years ago in ancient Israel), we can therefore add to and subtract from God's law in the way that seems to be most practical in our modern context. This is the same liberal line of reasoning that's used to justify rejecting male-only eldership in the local congregation on the basis that it was "cultural," even though St. Paul never argued like that either in 1 Timothy or Titus.

There are in fact two problems with this way of thinking. The first is that this line of reasoning is a form of what C.S. Lewis called, "chronological snobbery."[1] This is a logical fallacy. Why? It tries to argue that things newer are better than things more ancient simply because they are newer. For example, the prophet Samuel says that a state taxing 10 percent (the tithe) is a curse on a nation and evidence that it's trying to establish itself as the ultimate authority in the place of God (cf. 1 Samuel 8:15). Yet, due to our modern scientific and technological advancements, it's somehow now a necessity instead of a curse for the civil government to tax its citizens more than 10 percent. For the Bible-believing Christian, this ought to be a massive problem, for God cannot contradict Himself and is entirely consistent, since He Himself is the very definition of logic.

This brings us to the second problem with this mindset—situational ethics. By arguing that we can disregard or revamp ethical portions of what Yahweh has revealed in His Word, all on the basis that our situation today is different from that at the time of the biblical authors, we have denied the immutability (unchangeability) of God's moral law, and therefore also the immutability of the God Who gave it. It also denies the wise foreknowledge of God by treating His ethical standards as though He gave them in a historical vacuum without any view for how they would rightly be applied in every age from that point forward. Again, this mindset smacks of pride. Are we to think that we can somehow concoct moral principles superior to those of God Almighty for the building of culture, the governing of society, and the

---

[1] C.S. Lewis, *Surprised By Joy: The Shape of My Early Life*, New York: Harper Collins, 1955, pg. 207-208.

flourishing thereof? St. Paul writes to the Romans, "But who are you, O man, to answer back to God? Will what is molded say to its molder, 'Why have you made me like this?'" (Romans 9:20). While this was written in response to objections concerning unconditional election, the root principle here also applies to how we view God's law. Truly, where we find ourselves with this kind of arrogant attitude, we must repent in true contrition of heart and gladly submit our whole selves to the totality of His law-Word.

As we come to the conclusion of this work, it's important to underline again the main thrust. For some readers what I have written may be bone-rattlingly challenging, since it goes against many deeply held traditions within modern Christianity. Nevertheless, I do believe that for which I have argued throughout is the only way to be consistent with both *Sola Scriptura (Only Scripture)* and *Tota Scriptura (All of Scripture)*, striving to follow the way God's holy Word interprets itself. Indeed, we need both the authority of Scripture *and* the sufficiency of Scripture for all of life and doctrine. May this biblically derived framework of authority and ethics give us the proper foundation for envisioning a truly Christian social order. May it motivate us to passionately get involved in building culture around the Gospel of Jesus' kingdom-rule for His glory, including as it pertains to the governance thereof. May all the world know that there is only one, true head of state in Canada— and every other nation for that matter—to Whom is owed the absolute allegiance of all lesser authorities. His name is Jesus the Messiah and He alone is the true Ruler of kings on earth! May our motto ever be, "No King but Christ!" Amen and amen.

ABOUT THE AUTHOR

David A. Forsythe serves as an elder-pastor at Christ Covenant Church in Selkirk, Manitoba, Canada. He and his wife, Alyssa, are grateful to be raising six children together. David graduated from Peace River Bible Institute in 2012 with a focus in Global Ministries and has served in three countries on three continents, including ministry work in Malawi, Central Africa. He has also been active in public life, including running as a candidate in the 2022 Ontario provincial election, seeking to promote truth, justice, and the protection of those affected by government overreach.

9 7 9 8 9 9 9 1 6 9 3 2 8 8